Replicating & Reproducing Policing Research

This book addresses the need for policing scholarship to strengthen its empirical cumulative knowledge base by replicating and reproducing earlier studies.

The chapters in this volume advance policing research by replicating and reproducing earlier studies, investigating the generalizability of research findings, and making data and research methods available to other researchers to encourage scientific exploration of previous research findings. Each chapter addresses important scientific goals of validity, reliability, and generalizability, which build our cumulative knowledge of what is known in policing research, ultimately informing policymaking. This book offers insights into why replicating and reproducing policing scholarship is critical: from emphasizing the importance of making data and study material publicly available to facilitate replications and reproductions to reproducing studies in new contexts and cautioning against making policy-making decisions based on studies that have not been replicated.

This volume highlights the immense value in shifting researchers' priorities – even slightly – to focus less so on originality and innovation to make room for replications and reproductions, thereby shedding light on how true, empirical knowledge on policing and police practice is dependent on it. This book was originally published as a special issue of *Police Practice and Research.*

Khadija Monk is Assistant Professor in the School of Criminal Justice & Criminalistics at California State University, Los Angeles (Cal State LA), USA. She is also a liaison between Cal State LA and the Los Angeles Police Department's Police Orientation & Preparation Program (POPP). Dr. Monk's research interests include police-community relations, crime prevention, crime policy, and disparities in the criminal justice system. Her work has been published in *Crime & Delinquency*, the *Department of Justice's Office of Community Oriented Policing Services*, and the *International Journal of Police Strategies & Management.*

Jacek Koziarski earned his Ph.D. from the Sociology Department at the University of Western Ontario, London, Canada, and his B.A. and M.A. degrees in Criminology from the Faculty of Social Science and Humanities at the University of Ontario Institute of Technology, Oshawa, Canada. Jacek's research centers on various aspects of policing, with a particular focus on police interactions with persons with perceived mental illness. Another line of inquiry for Jacek's work centers around examining the spatial and temporal patterns of both crime- and non-crime-related policing issues. Some of his research appears in peer-reviewed outlets such as *Crime Science*, *Policing: A Journal of Policy and Practice*, and *Criminology & Public Policy.*

Replicating & Reproducing Policing Research

Edited by
Khadija Monk and Jacek Koziarski

Routledge
Taylor & Francis Group
LONDON AND NEW YORK

First published 2024
by Routledge
4 Park Square, Milton Park, Abingdon, Oxon, OX14 4RN

and by Routledge
605 Third Avenue, New York, NY 10158

Routledge is an imprint of the Taylor & Francis Group, an informa business

British Library Cataloguing-in-Publication Data
A catalogue record for this book is available from the British Library

ISBN13: 978-1-032-71208-6 (hbk)
ISBN13: 978-1-032-71211-6 (pbk)
ISBN13: 978-1-032-71213-0 (ebk)

DOI: 10.4324/9781032712130

Typeset in Minion Pro
by codeMantra

Publisher's Note
The publisher accepts responsibility for any inconsistencies that may have arisen during the conversion of this book from journal articles to book chapters, namely the inclusion of journal terminology.

Contents

Citation Information

The chapters in this book were originally published in the journal *Police Practice and Research*, volume 24, issue 5 (2023). When citing this material, please use the original page numbering for each article, as follows:

Introduction

Replicating & reproducing policing research
Khadija Monk and Jacek Koziarski
Police Practice and Research, volume 24, issue 5 (2023), pp. 519–522

Chapter 1

Describing the scale and composition of calls for police service: a replication and extension using open data
Samuel Langton, Stijn Ruiter and Tim Verlaan
Police Practice and Research, volume 24, issue 5 (2023), pp. 523–538

Chapter 2

A street segment analysis of crime in a township: evidence from South Africa
Kayla Theron, Gregory Dennis Breetzke, Lourens Snyman and Ian Edelstein
Police Practice and Research, volume 24, issue 5 (2023), pp. 539–557

Chapter 3

A qualitative exploration of stress in a criminal investigations section
Kathleen E. Padilla, Alexis R. Rockwell and Jessica Huff
Police Practice and Research, volume 24, issue 5 (2023), pp. 558–574

Chapter 4

Examining the effects of the killing of George Floyd by police in the United States on attitudes of Black Londoners: a replication
Amy Nivette, Christof Nägel and Emily Gilbert
Police Practice and Research, volume 24, issue 5 (2023), pp. 575–596

Chapter 5

How generalizable are findings from police surveys? A review of multi-agency studies
Erin M. Kearns and Justin Nix
Police Practice and Research, volume 24, issue 5 (2023), pp. 597–611

Notes on Contributors

Gregory Dennis Breetzke is Associate Professor in the Department of Geography, Geoinformatics and Meteorology at the University of Pretoria, Africa. He is a spatial crime researcher whose research focuses on the geospatial analysis of crime and criminal offenders. He is particularly interested in examining crime patterns and trends and how they vary across space and time. Other current interests include the development of indigenous theories of crime and the examination of crime as a development issue.

Ian Edelstein holds a Ph.D. in Sociology from the University of Cape Town, South Africa, and a Masters in Public Administration from Syracuse University, USA. He currently works for the Washington State Department of Children, Youth & Families to improve evidence-based decision-making. He completed a postdoctoral fellowship in the Research Use and Impact Assessment Unit of the Human Sciences Research Council in Pretoria, South Africa. His areas of research interest include interpersonal violence, youth development/sport-based development, programme evaluation/impact assessment, education reform, and poverty/inequality studies.

Emily Gilbert is Principal Research Officer at the London Mayor's Office for Policing And Crime (MOPAC). She gained her Ph.D. in Survey Methodology from the University of Essex, UK. Her research interests include attitude measurement, data quality, and the use of new technology and innovative methods for data collection, as well as public perceptions of the police.

Jessica Huff is Assistant Professor in the School of Criminology and Criminal Justice at the University of Nebraska Omaha, USA. She uses experimental methods to examine police programs and policies to identify what works and how to ensure equitable police encounters with diverse populations. She is NIJ LEADS Academic who has partnered with police agencies across the U.S. to evaluate programs, including body-worn cameras and violence reduction strategies. Her work has been funded by the Department of Homeland Security, Centers for Disease Control and Prevention, and the Bureau of Justice Assistance.

Erin M. Kearns is Director of Prevention Research Initiatives at the National Counterterrorism Innovation, Technology, and Education (NCITE) Center and Associate Professor in the School of Criminology and Criminal Justice at the University of Nebraska Omaha, USA. Her research on terrorism, media, and community-police relations has been funded through several sources and featured on numerous media outlets.

Jacek Koziarski earned his Ph.D. from the Sociology Department at the University of Western Ontario, London, Canada, and his B.A. and M.A. degrees in Criminology from the Faculty of Social Science and Humanities at the University of Ontario Institute of Technology, Oshawa, Canada. Jacek's research centers on various aspects of policing, with a particular focus on police interactions with persons with perceived mental illness. Another line of inquiry for Jacek's work centers around examining the spatial and temporal patterns of both crime- and non-crime-related policing issues. Some of his research appears in peer-reviewed outlets such as *Crime Science*, *Policing: A Journal of Policy and Practice*, and *Criminology & Public Policy*.

Samuel Langton is a postdoctoral researcher in evidence-based policing at the Netherlands Institute for the Study of Crime and Law Enforcement. His research focuses on describing and explaining the spatial and temporal patterning of demand for police services in the Netherlands. Sam is also interested in promoting open science in crime and policing research.

Khadija Monk is Assistant Professor in the School of Criminal Justice & Criminalistics at California State University, Los Angeles (Cal State LA). She is also a liaison between Cal State LA and the Los Angeles Police Department's Police Orientation & Preparation Program (POPP). Dr. Monk's research interests include police-community relations, crime prevention, crime policy, and disparities in the criminal justice system. Her work has been published in *Crime & Delinquency*, the *Department of Justice's Office of Community Oriented Policing Services*, and the *International Journal of Police Strategies & Management*.

Christof Nägel is a postdoctoral researcher at the University of Cologne, Germany. His research and teaching areas include causes and consequences of police misconduct, as well as methods of causal inference in criminological research.

Amy Nivette is Associate Professor at Utrecht University, the Netherlands. Her research interests include the determinants of institutional legitimacy and attitudes toward the law over the life course, with a particular focus on what social, experiential, and individual factors shape attitudes towards the police. She is also Research Fellow at the Netherlands Institute for the Study of Crime and Law Enforcement.

Justin Nix is Distinguished Associate Professor in the School of Criminology and Criminal Justice at the University of Nebraska Omaha, USA, where he researches police legitimacy, procedural justice, and police shootings. He was the 2020 recipient of the Early Career Award from the American Society of Criminology's Division of Policing. His recent work appears in *Justice Quarterly*, *Criminology and Public Policy*, and *Criminology*.

Kathleen E. Padilla is Assistant Professor in the School of Criminal Justice & Criminology at Texas State University, USA. Kathleen received her Ph.D. in Criminology & Criminal Justice from Arizona State University, Tempe, USA. Her research interests include police officer health and wellness, police officer perceptions, qualitative methodology, and juvenile justice. Her work has appeared in *Occupational Medicine*; *Psychology, Public Policy, and Law*; and *Journal of Experimental Criminology*.

Alexis R. Rockwell is Assistant Professor in the Department of Political Science and Criminal Justice at the University of South Alabama, Mobile, USA. Alexis received her Ph.D. in Criminal Justice from Sam Houston State University, Huntsville, USA. Her research interests include police culture and police policies, including body-worn camera and the use of force policies. Her research utilizes both quantitative and qualitative methodologies. Her recent work has appeared in *Policing: An International Journal* and *Policing: A Journal of Policy and Practice.*

Stijn Ruiter is Senior Researcher at the Netherlands Institute for the Study of Crime and Law Enforcement. He is also Professor at the Department of Sociology at Utrecht University, the Netherlands. Stijn's research interests include geographic/environmental criminology, evidence-based policing, quantitative/analytical sociology, and open science.

Lourens Snyman is Senior Cartographer (Geospatial Information Services) in the Department of Geography, Geoinformatics and Meteorology at the University of Pretoria, South Africa. He is also a current doctoral student in the department with research interests in geographic accessibility, spatial behavioural economics, and map visualization.

Kayla Theron is a post-graduate Geoinformatics student in the Department of Geography, Geoinformatics and Meteorology at the University of Pretoria, South Africa. Her research focuses on examining the factors that increase the risk of crime across transportation routes.

Tim Verlaan is a Ph.D. candidate in evidence-based policing at the Netherlands Institute for the Study of Crime and Law Enforcement. His research focuses on modelling the demand and supply for police services in the Netherlands.

Introduction to replicating & reproducing policing research

Khadija Monk and Jacek Koziarski

In science, replication and reproduction are critical for understanding the reliability of findings from scholarship that came before. When an independent group of researchers collects new data with the intention to replicate an earlier study and end up drawing similar conclusions, our certainty in knowing or understanding the phenomenon under scientific scrutiny grows; if, on the other hand, a replication fails to draw similar conclusions, what we know or understand about the phenomenon under scientific scrutiny is rightfully called into question (Lamal, 1990; Popper, 2005; Simons, 2014). As such, replication and reproduction in science is not only critical for knowledge creation, but for *verifying* what we know as well.

Despite serving as critical pillars in the creation and verification of scientific knowledge, however, some fields do not engage in replication or reproduction efforts regularly. Psychology, for example, has been experiencing a so-called 'replication crisis' for the better part of the last two decades after researchers not only realized that few studies in the field have been replicated or reproduced, but when replications or reproductions were attempted, they were either not possible to conduct or failed to draw conclusions that were similar to their original investigations (Makel et al., 2012; Maxwell et al., 2015). The picture of replication and reproduction in criminology, and indeed the sub-field of policing, are no different. An investigation by McNeeley and Warner (2015), for example, found that between 2006 and 2010, just over 2% of published criminological studies were replications. And in policing, with exception to a small list of police practices that have received considerable empirical attention – such as hot spots policing (e.g., Braga et al., 2019) – policing scholarship has largely not faced the scrutiny of subsequent replication or reproduction efforts either. As such, whether replications or reproductions of existing policing scholarship can yield conclusions similar to their original investigations, let alone whether replications or reproductions of existing policing scholarship are even possible to begin with, remains to be seen.

While an Editorial Introduction is not the appropriate venue to unpack the many reasons for why a replication crisis, too, exists in the field of policing, we would like to briefly touch upon one of these reasons: a bias toward publishing scholarship that is new, original, and innovative (Huey & Bennell, 2017). This bias is likely influenced by the fact that policing as an academic field is still 'new', so there is still a considerable amount of the profession that has been untapped for empirical investigation. Indeed, Discussion sections published in across policing journals – including this one – often contain a laundry list of related areas in need of future research because there is much more left to explore. Additionally, with the police possessing a broad net of roles and responsibilities that are not firmly defined (see e.g., Langton et al., 2022; Lum et al., 2022), the police as an institution and policing as a practice are constantly developing and evolving to meet the demand for their services with new opportunities for empirical investigation arising in tandem.

To be clear: new, original, and innovative scholarship that broadens and expands our current understanding of policing is needed and should continue to be encouraged. However, policing scholars should not be putting all their eggs into the baskets of 'originality' and 'innovation', so-to-speak. As Lowenkamp et al. (2003, p. 353) explains, continuing to do so can be detrimental:

> Breaking new theoretical and/or empirical ground is perhaps of prime importance, for such efforts potentially push the field to new horizons. Nevertheless, the emphasis on innovation over systematic replication has a cost: the inability to build cumulative knowledge and to be able to state with confidence what is, and is not, known.

And while the field of policing has much work to do towards increasing the confidence in what is and is not known, this Special Issue, comprised of five manuscripts that either seek to replicate or reproduce earlier studies or investigate the generalizability of research findings, is a small step toward a re-balancing of empirical priorities in policing.

In light of recent interest in the roles and responsibilities of the police and demand on police resources, Langton et al. (2022) replicated earlier work from Ratcliffe (2021) and Lum et al. (2022) to understand the scale and composition of calls for service in Detroit, Michigan. Similar to the scholarship that Langton et al. (2022) were guided by, they not only found that the police are expected to fulfill social and crime-fighting functions, but that certain calls for service account for a disproportionate amount of police officer time. Importantly, Langton et al. (2022) provide a pathway to replication and reproduction for other researchers by using open-source data along with open study materials. By making their data and analytic plan publicly available, they are encouraging replication and reproduction of their study, which would add to the validity and robustness of their findings.

Theron et al. (2022) conducted an analysis of crime concentration, with a focus on how their findings can be used to inform the deployment of police resources. While the concentration of crime is a well-understood phenomenon – even leading Weisburd (2015) to posit a *Law of Crime Concentration*—most of our understanding on this issue comes from jurisdictions located in Western countries – findings from which may or may not be generalizable to other contexts. North American and European studies on this topic, for example, not only aggregate their data into census tracts or other administrative spatial boundaries that may not exist elsewhere, but they are also based in contexts that may have different cultural and geopolitical norms than developing nations, therefore further limiting the generalizability of Western studies to other parts of the world. Theron et al. (2022) contribution, on the other hand, expanded this literature into Khayelitsha, South Africa – a largely informal township with shacks and no formal street addresses. Specifically, they investigated crime concentration across street segments in Khayelitsha and concluded that – like previous scholarship (see e.g., Weisburd & Amram, 2014) – crime is considerably concentrated across street segments in this township as well. They argue that their findings are important for informing the efficient deployment of police services – an approach they note is particularly important for their study context given scarce police resources.

Padilla et al. (2023) conducted a qualitative replication of Dabney et al. (2013), who examined stress experienced by police investigators. While the sample of investigators differed between the two studies, and the police organizations differed demographically and operationally as well, Padilla et al. (2023) note that investigators in both studies endured many of the same stressors, thus replicating the findings of Dabney et al. (2013). While qualitative work is not driven or influenced by the goal of generalizability, further efforts as those by Padilla et al. (2023) are needed to highlight important commonalities that exist in the voices of police practitioners.

Nivette et al. (2023) examined the effect that the murder of George Floyd had on the attitudes of Black residents towards the police in London, England. More specifically, a study by Laniyonu (2021) found that the death of Eric Garner led to Black Londoners having a significantly lower level of support for the Metropolitan Police; Nivette et al. (2023) sought to uncover whether this transnational effect replicated following the murder of George Floyd. In contrast to their hypothesis, Nivette et al. (2023) found that the murder of George Floyd had no immediate effect on Londoners' attitudes toward the police, regardless of ethnicity. When a longer temporal period was considered instead, Nivette et al. (2023) found that Londoners' attitudes towards the police were more negative overall after the murder of George Floyd, but unrelated issues that were on-going simultaneously – such as the COVID-19 pandemic and the policing of public health restrictions – impacted their ability to conclude whether the increase in negative attitudes was due to the murder of George Floyd or other factors.

Finally, Kearns and Nix (2023) argue that due to issues around access, policing surveys often reflect the perspective of a single organization, meaning that the generalizability of such police surveys is not known. In an attempt to unpack this issue, Kearns and Nix (2023) reviewed data from 15 studies which collected survey data from more than one policing organization to examine whether findings were consistent across organizations. They found results were consistent across organizations in just one study, with the remaining studies showing either partial replication of results or results that were in complete contrast to those from other police organizations that were sampled. In light of their findings, Kearns and Nix (2023) caution against policy-making that is informed by research from a single police organization and emphasize the need for replications.

Altogether, this Special Issue provides only a small glimpse into why replicating and reproducing policing scholarship is critical; from emphasizing the importance of making data and study material publicly available to facilitate replications and reproductions, to reproducing studies in new contexts and cautions against making policy-making decisions based on studies that have not been replicated, there is immense value in shifting researchers' priorities – even slightly – to focus less so on originality and innovation to make room for replications and reproductions. True, empirical knowledge on policing and police practice is dependent on it. Given the contributions to this Special Issue, however, we are optimistic that the field has what it takes to make the necessary priority shift and we look forward toward seeing what the future holds for policing scholarship.

Disclosure statement

No potential conflict of interest was reported by the authors.

References

Braga, A. A., Turchan, B. S., Papachristos, A. V., & Hureau, D. M. (2019). Hot spots policing and crime reduction: An update of an ongoing systematic review and meta-analysis. *Journal of Experimental Criminology*, *15*(3), 289–311. https://doi.org/10.1007/s11292-019-09372-3

Dabney, D. A., Copes, H., Tewksbury, R., & Hawk-Tourtelot, S. R. (2013). A qualitative assessment of stress perceptions among members of a homicide unit. *Justice Quarterly*, *30*(5), 811–836. https://doi.org/10.1080/07418825.2011.633542

Huey, L., & Bennell, C. (2017). Replication and reproduction in Canadian policing research: A note. *Canadian Journal of Criminology and Criminal Justice*, *59*(1), 123–138. https://doi.org/10.3138/cjccj.2016.E09

Kearns, E. M., & Nix, J. (2023). How generalizable are findings from police surveys?: A review of multi-agency studies. *Police Practice & Research*, 1–15. https://doi.org/10.1080/15614263.2023.2214282

Lamal, P. A. (1990). On the importance of replication. *Journal of Social Behavior and Personality*, *5*(4), 31.

Langton, S., Ruiter, S., & Verlaan, T. (2022). Describing the scale and composition of calls for police service: A replication and extension using open data. *Police Practice & Research*, 1–16. https://doi.org/10.1080/15614263.2022.2102494

Laniyonu, A. (2021). Phantom pains: The effect of police killings of Black Americans on Black British Attitudes. *British Journal of Political Science*, *52*(4), 1651–1667. https://doi.org/10.1017/S0007123421000557

Lowenkamp, C. T., Cullen, F. T., & Pratt, T. C. (2003). Replicating Sampson and Groves's test of social disorganization theory: Revisiting a criminological classic. *Journal of Research in Crime and Delinquency*, *40*(4), 351–373. https://doi.org/10.1177/0022427803256077

Lum, C., Koper, C. S., & Wu, X. (2022). Can we really defund the police? A nine-agency study of police response to calls for service. *Police Quarterly*, *25*(3), 255–280. https://doi.org/10.1177/10986111211035002

Makel, M. C., Plucker, J. A., & Hegarty, B. (2012). Replications in psychology research: How often do they really occur? *Perspectives on Psychological Science*, *7*(6), 537–542. https://doi.org/10.1177/1745691612460688

Maxwell, S. E., Lau, M. Y., & Howard, G. S. (2015). Is psychology suffering from a replication crisis? What does "failure to replicate" really mean? *American Psychologist*, *70*(6), 487–498. https://doi.org/10.1037/a0039400

McNeeley, S., & Warner, J. J. (2015). Replication in criminology: A necessary practice. *European Journal of Criminology*, *12*(5), 581–597. https://doi.org/10.1177/1477370815578197

Nivette, A., Nägel, C., & Gilbert, E. (2023). Examining the effects of the killing of George Floyd by police in the United States on attitudes of Black Londoners: A replication. *Police Practice & Research*, 1–22. https://doi.org/10.1080/15614263.2023.2185241

Padilla, K. E., Rockwell, A. R., & Huff, J. (2023). A qualitative exploration of stress in a criminal investigations section. *Police Practice & Research*, 1–17. https://doi.org/10.1080/15614263.2023.2185242

Popper, K. (2005). *The logic of scientific discovery*. Routledge.

Ratcliffe, J. (2021). Policing and public health calls for service in Philadelphia. *Crime Science*, *10*(5). https://doi.org/10.1186/s40163-021-00141-0

Simons, D. J. (2014). The value of direct replication. *Perspectives on Psychological Science*, *9*(1), 76–80. https://doi.org/10.1177/1745691613514755

Theron, K., Breetzke, G. D., Snyman, L., & Edelstein, I. (2022). A street segment analysis of crime in a township: Evidence from South Africa. *Police Practice & Research*, 1–19. https://doi.org/10.1080/15614263.2022.2147070

Weisburd, D. (2015). The law of crime concentration and the criminology of place. *Criminology*, *53*(2), 133–157. https://doi.org/10.1111/1745-9125.12070

Weisburd, D., & Amram, S. (2014). The law of concentrations of crime at place: The case of Tel Aviv-Jaffa. *Police Practice & Research*, *15*(2), 101–114. https://doi.org/10.1080/15614263.2013.874169

Khadija Monk

Jacek Koziarski

Describing the scale and composition of calls for police service: a replication and extension using open data

Samuel Langton, Stijn Ruiter and Tim Verlaan

ABSTRACT

This paper describes the scale and composition of emergency demand for police services in Detroit, United States. The contribution is made in replication and extension of analyses reported elsewhere in the United States. Findings indicate that police spend a considerable proportion of time performing a social service function. Just 51% of the total deployed time responding to 911 calls is consumed by crime incidents. The remainder is spent on quality of life (16%), traffic (15%), health (7%), community (5%), and proactive (4%) duties. A small number of incidents consume a disproportionately large amount of police officer time. Emergency demand is concentrated in time and space, and can differ between types of demand. The findings further highlight the potential implications of radically reforming police forces in the United States. The data and code used here are openly available for reproduction, reuse, and scrutiny.

1 Background

Amidst austerity measures, growing public expectation, and scrutiny, understanding the public demand for police services has become a priority among evidence-based policing researchers and practitioners (Boulton et al., 2017). Without a grasp on the scale ('how much?') and composition ('what type?') of police demand, we are likely to observe suboptimal and inequitable outcomes for the public, the inappropriate distribution of public funds, and unnecessary strain on officers (Ellison et al., 2021; Lum et al., 2021). Understanding the characteristics of public demand for the police has become particularly pertinent following recent calls to rethink, and in some cases, radically reform, the role and reach of contemporary police forces (Lum et al., 2021). Despite the importance of this topic, and the public interest invested in the findings, we are currently lacking open replications and extensions of existing research. This study represents the first such investigation using open data from Detroit, United States, to replicate and extend recent analyses presented by Ratcliffe (2021) and Lum et al. (2021). It also presents open study materials which can be used to reproduce the results and replicate analyses across different contexts.

Ratcliffe (2021) sought to describe the complexity and diversity of public demand for police services in Philadelphia, United States (US), during 2019. The study was motivated by the recognition that police spend a considerable proportion of deployed resource resolving incidents which fall outside of the traditional crime-fighting role of the police. Instead, the origins of public demand for the police can often be attributed to a lack of supply and/or accessibility failure in other organizations, such as those providing support for people requiring (mental) health assistance (van dijk & crofts, 2017; Wood et al., 2021). Ratcliffe reported that just 40% of public emergency calls for service during the year were crime incidents. These calls consumed 55% of the total officer shift time. The remaining public demand from calls involved community issues (10% of calls, 7% of time), medical/public health incidents (7% of calls, 9% of time), proactive policing (8% of calls, 5% of time), quality of life (24% of calls, 14% of time), and traffic duties (11% of calls and 11% of time). Comparable results were subsequently reported across multiple anonymized police jurisdictions in the US (Lum et al., 2021; see also, Lum & Koper, 2021 in *The Washington Post*).

These descriptive findings provided data-driven evidence to suggest that the police indeed spend considerable amounts of time dealing with incidents in a social rather than solely crime-fighting capacity. This has implications to and beyond policing practice. The findings directly contribute to the fierce and politically charged debates around the role and responsibilities of police officers in contemporary society. Both Ratcliffe (2021) and Lum et al. (2021) were published amidst the backdrop of the killing of George Floyd in May 2020 and subsequent 'defund the police' protests across the US. Evidence which demonstrates that the public relies on the police for social duties beyond law enforcement suggests that a radical reduction in their role and responsibilities (e.g., through defunding) would increase demand on other social services. Should such radical reform take place without first understanding the scale and composition of public demand for the police, and without preemptively providing appropriate substitutes, there will be no supply to meet this shift in demand. Thus, Ratcliffe (2021) and Lum et al. (2021) contributed important empirical data to the (ongoing) discussion on police reform in the US.

Here, we propose an extension of Ratcliffe (2021) and Lum et al. (2021). This extension has two principal components. First, we replicate the main analyses of these existing investigations into the scale and composition of police demand using open study materials. To date, investigations have been conducted on data which are not publicly available and without the materials (e.g., code) to reproduce the results. Open science practices have been identified as fundamental to the aims of evidence-based policing and vital in ensuring that in the long term, real-life decisions are based on a concrete and replicable pool of evidence (Bennell & Blaskovits, 2019). Yet, reproductions and replications are rare. This has been demonstrated in domestic policing research (Huey & Bennell, 2017) and criminology more broadly (McNeeley & Warner, 2015). The necessity for a fully open investigation into the scale and composition of police demand is particularly important given the public nature of the debate around police reform and the considerable implications of redefining the role of the police without transparent empirical investigation. It is reasonable for police practitioners and the public to expect a thorough, open, and replicable investigation into police demand before academia concludes that the issue is resolved – certainly, before findings are used to change or introduce police practice or public policy. Open materials have the additional benefit of being available for reuse in other jurisdictions, helping build a reliable and comparable evidence-base around the scale and composition of police demand across different contexts.

Second, we extend the analyses used by Ratcliffe (2021) and Lum et al. (2021). This includes a comparison between measures of officer time with and without the response time. While Lum and colleagues raised concerns about the inclusion of the response time in measures of officer time, largely due to low-priority calls not necessitating a rapid response, the precise impact of their usage on the same data is unclear. We also provide a comprehensive account of the variability in the time consumed by different demand classifications (e.g., crime, community, health). These statistics shed light on the degree to which a disproportionately large amount of officer time is consumed by just a small number of calls – insight which can be used to assess how a reduction in demand, or a shift away from calls for police service towards other social services, might free-up officer time. In addition, we report on the spatial and temporal patterning of each demand classification. Distinctions in these patterns across demand types would be indicative of similarly distinct demand-generating mechanisms (e.g., built environment). Such concentrations in time and space might also inform deployment decisions based on officer expertise and experience, and/or collaboration with other services, such as mental health professionals (e.g., White & Weisburd, 2018).

With these points in mind, this paper describes the emergency demand for police services in a large city, Detroit, US, using open data and open code. All materials are publicly available (see https://github.com/langtonhugh/demand_detroit). It does so in replication, and where appropriate extension, of the main findings reported by Ratcliffe (2021) and later Lum et al. (2021). In this way, the contribution serves to test the robustness of existing findings; provides the materials required for reuse, reproduction, and replication; and provides additional insight through new analyses.

2 Describing demand

Given the aims of this study, this section first provides a brief outline of the data and methods used by Ratcliffe (2021) and Lum et al. (2021) to describe the scale and composition of emergency reactive police demand.

2.1 Ratcliffe (2021)

Using computer-aided dispatch (CAD) data from the Philadelphia Police Department (PPD), the Ratcliffe (2021) study provided a breakdown of calls for police service during 2019. Calls were subset to exclude those which did not require officer dispatch or did not originate from the public. CAD codes, discrete descriptions of incidents based on information available to the dispatcher, were categorized into six broad classifications: community issues, crime, medical/public health, proactive policing, quality of life, and traffic duties. The classification scheme was used to report on the frequency and proportional breakdown of calls relating to each type of demand throughout 2019.

Recognizing that frequency counts of calls for service do not necessarily reflect the amount of police resource consumed by public demand, raw counts were augmented with the time spent by officers on each of the six classifications of demand. This information permits the calculation of a proportional breakdown of police time consumed by the different demand classifications throughout the year. The raw numbers were reported in a table. A visual representation of call types nested within each demand classification was summarized in a tree map graphic. The time committed by officers was calculated from when the call was dispatched to an officer to when the officer indicated that the event had been closed. Ratcliffe accounted for the number of officers attending each incident when calculating the amount of time consumed. The aggregate time consumed by different demand classifications was reported using a single count of officer shifts (7.5 hours) over the year.

The spatio-temporal patterning of this demand was summarized in two visuals, focusing specifically on those calls relating to medical/public health. A heatmap showed the mean call volume during hours of the day and days of the week, identifying peak times for demand. A geographic map visualized the spatial patterning of these call count concentrations using kernel density estimation in order to identify hotspots of police demand involving medical/public health issues. To supplement these findings, Ratcliffe also reported on the differences between the initial CAD incident type classification and the final disposition using a Sankey diagram – again focusing specifically on medical and public health calls.

2.2 Lum et al. *(2021)*

To describe the scale and composition of emergency police demand across the US more broadly, Lum et al. (2021) used CAD data from nine different police agencies. The agencies themselves were anonymized. Individual incidents were categorized into 14 different demand classifications, namely, alarms, disorders, vice, domestic, follow-ups and service requests, mental, medical, missing persons, violence, interpersonal-other, property, suspicions, traffic, and admin, agency, and non-crime. The authors reported a proportional breakdown of call counts and police time spent across the nine agencies according to the 14 demand classifications, including the average (mean). For each agency, the authors also reported the average time spent on each demand classification in minutes, and the average across the nine agencies. No descriptive statistics on the range or spread of these figures was reported.

The 'time spent' measure used was the *time on scene* (i.e., excluding the response time). The authors considered this to be preferable since low priority calls may have a non-urgent (slow) response due to the nature of the call, and officers may be reassigned to other duties while on an assignment. Lum and colleagues calculated the *time on scene* as the time from the first officer's arrival to when the call was reported as resolved. In this way, the calculation did not account for the additional time consumed by multi-officer responses (e.g., backup). This was justified for a number of reasons, among them, avoiding the over-inflation of time estimates due to multiple officers attending non-serious incidents, and limitations with the CAD data. A proportional breakdown of the disposition (assist only, report written or arrest citation) was provided for each of the 14 call types. No spatial or temporal findings were reported.

3 Data

3.1 Detroit calls for service

The data used for this study cover the city of Detroit in Michigan, US. The City of Detroit authority publish 911 emergency calls for service data through their Open Data Portal.[1] In alignment with the two existing studies, the data used here exclude those calls initiated by an officer in order to capture public-initiated calls. Each individual incident has a corresponding timestamp and location coordinates to define it in time and space. Data was a subset for the year 2019.

For each incident, the police response time and time on the scene are reported. The former measures the time from dispatch to when the first officer arrives on-scene.[2] The latter mimics the measure used by Lum et al. (2021), namely, the amount of time which elapses between when the first officer arrives and when the last unit clears the scene. Here, the data permit a distinction between the time spent on calls with and without the response time. We refer to the sum of the response time and time on scene as the *total deployed time*. Calls which had a response time of negative values or missing were dropped from analyses. Calls which had a *time on scene* of 0 minutes, negative values or missing were also excluded. As noted, Lum et al. (2021) considered the *time on scene* measure to be preferable. For completeness, in this study, we report times with and without the response time – defined as travel time.

Each incident has a *call description* variable which describes the nature of the call. Call descriptions involving administrative duties (e.g., 'start of shift information'), completely unknown problems, and non-deployment (e.g., 'employee call in/time off') were removed. This left 207 unique call description categories. In the interests of parsimony and ease of interpretation, these categories were recoded into 99 broader call descriptions.[3] This included the removal of incidents involving transporting prisoners and executing warrants, which were deemed to have been erroneously flagged as not being officer-initiated. Each call description was then categorized into the six demand-type classifications used in Ratcliffe (2021), namely, crime, community, medical/public health, proactive, quality of life, and traffic. A total of 2.8% of calls were deemed unclassifiable. For each of the six demand classifications, an 'other' incident type was generated for those incidents which consumed less than 0.2% of the total deployed time during the year. This left a total of 49 unique categories for the reported breakdowns, capturing ~260,000 individual public calls for service in Detroit during 2019. No information on the final disposition of calls is provided in the open data.

4 Methods

The methods used largely replicate those used by Ratcliffe (2021) and Lum et al. (2021), and where appropriate, extensions. First, descriptive statistics and a treemap graphic provide an account of the scale and composition of police demand during the year. Second, visualizations summarize the spatial and temporal patterning of this demand.

4.1 Descriptive statistics

Summary statistics describe the overall composition of demand according to the six demand-type classifications. This includes call frequency counts, a proportional breakdown of call counts, and a proportional breakdown of police time. Both *total deployed time* (response time + time on scene) and *time on scene* measures of police resource are reported. The proportional breakdown of *time on scene* is visualized using a treemap graphic for each incident type nested within the demand classifications. The equivalent graphic for *total deployed time* is available in the corresponding GitHub repository.

A series of descriptive statistics summarize the time on scene consumed by each demand type. For comprehensiveness and transparency, we report the mean, median, standard deviation, and range, and in the Appendix, a histogram of the underlying distribution Figure 6. This sheds on light on how long a 'typical' call might take while noting a probable skew in the distribution. Such a skew would suggest that averages of time (e.g., Lum et al., 2021) or aggregate measures of time (e.g., Ratcliffe, 2021) in isolation are insufficient and potentially mask important underlying variation, namely, that a small number of high-demand calls drag up the mean and inflate aggregate measures of time. To investigate this distribution, we plot Lorenz curves for each demand classification. Lorenz curves plot the cumulative distribution of a variable (in this case, time on scene) against the cumulative distribution of a unit (in this case, incidents; Bernasco & Steenbeek, 2017). By way of example, we report on these figures according to thresholds of 25% and 50% of time spent. Here, we recognize that the thresholds are arbitrary, but their usage provides an interpretable metric for demonstrating the degree to which a disproportionately large amount of officer time might be consumed by just a small number of calls.

4.2 Spatio-temporal patterning

The temporal patterning of the six demand-type classifications are visualized using a heatmap of mean call counts, aggregated by day of the week, and hour of the day. To summarize the spatial patterning, call location coordinates are aggregated to synthetic grid cells using spatial joins. Grid cells are defined as 1000 ft^2 (305 m^2) – a size deemed appropriate based on a balance between capturing localized variation and interpretable visualizations. Two percent of incidents are excluded from the spatial visualizations due to incomplete geographic information. To accurately convey the resource deployed to each area during the year, maps visualize the aggregate *time on scene* (in hours) within each grid cell over the course of the year for each demand-type classification. The equivalent raw count maps are available in the Appendix, Figure 5. In this way, we visualize the spatio-temporal patterning of demand in a manner comparable to Ratcliffe (2021), while adding a comparison across different demand classifications and two different measures of demand.

5 Results

5.1 Scale and composition

The frequency counts and proportional breakdowns for each demand-type classification are reported in Table 1. This demonstrates that in Detroit, a considerable proportion of calls for service, and in turn, time spent by officers, is committed to a diverse array of (often non-criminal) issues.

Table 1. Breakdown of frequency counts and time spent on each demand type. Total deployed time is the sum of the time on scene and response time.

Demand type	Count	Count (%)	Time on scene (%)	Total deployed time (%)
community	14,466	5.59	5.06	5.15
crime	114,800	44.36	51.40	50.55
health	19,873	7.68	7.10	7.19
proactive	15,663	6.05	3.89	4.04
quality of life	54,702	21.14	14.66	15.54
traffic	32,147	12.42	15.63	15.27
unclassified	7135	2.76	2.25	2.26

Just 44% of emergency calls for service related to crime incidents. These crime incidents consume 51% of time on the scene throughout the year. The remainder of time on scene is spent dealing with traffic duties (16%), quality of life incidents (15%), public and mental health (7%), community issues (5%), and proactive policing (4%). The differences in the proportional breakdown between time on scene and total deployment time, which includes response time, are marginal. This indicates that the response time – as measured by travel time – plays only a minor role in determining the scale and composition of the time consumed.

The proportional breakdown of time spent on scene for each incident type, grouped by the six demand classifications, is visualized in Figure 1. [4] This figure demonstrates the diversity and complexity of public demand for police services in Detroit. Time consumed on the scene of crime incidents is largely comprised of domestic incidents, burglary, and assault. For traffic incidents, police time was mostly spent attending to accidents, while for quality of life, attending to disturbances consumed the most time on scene. Calls relating to public health involved mental health incidents, overdoses, (threats of) suicide, and well-being checks. Proactive incidents largely involved investigations, while time consumed on community issues consisted mostly of missing/found persons and animal incidents (e.g., aggressive dogs).

5.2 Time distributions

To further quantify the resources consumed, Table 2 summarizes the time spent on the scene for each demand classification in minutes. Histograms of the underlying distributions are reported in the Appendix. Table 2 demonstrates a number of things. First, there is a modest amount of variation in the typical time at the scene of different types of emergency calls. For instance, the mean time spent on the scene of traffic incidents (55 minutes) and crime (51 minutes) is considerably more than that of quality of life issues (31 minutes) or proactive activity (28 minutes). These differences will be a result of a combination of factors, including the complexity and severity of incidents. Second, there is considerable variation in the time consumed by incidents *within* each demand type. While many calls are resolved in minutes, a handful consume hours of officer time on the scene, resulting in a highly skewed distribution. This also highlights how mean or aggregate summary statistics of police time as a measure of demand can mask (important) underlying variation.

Figure 2 visualizes the disproportionate share of time spent on a small number of calls explicitly using Lorenz curves for each demand classification. These can be compared against the reference line of perfect equality. Here, the line of perfect equality represents a situation in which officer time is distributed evenly across all calls. In reality, we can see that this is not the case: the Lorenz curves for each demand classification deviate considerably from perfect equality. The curves for each classification are almost indistinguishable, so we focus on the curve for all calls (in blue). This shows that 50% of the time officers spent on the scene during 2019 was consumed by just 15% of calls, and 25% of time on scene was consumed by just 5% of all calls. In other words, a small number of emergency calls for service account for a disproportionately large amount of police resources out on the street. This finding is consistent (and comparable) across all six classifications of demand.

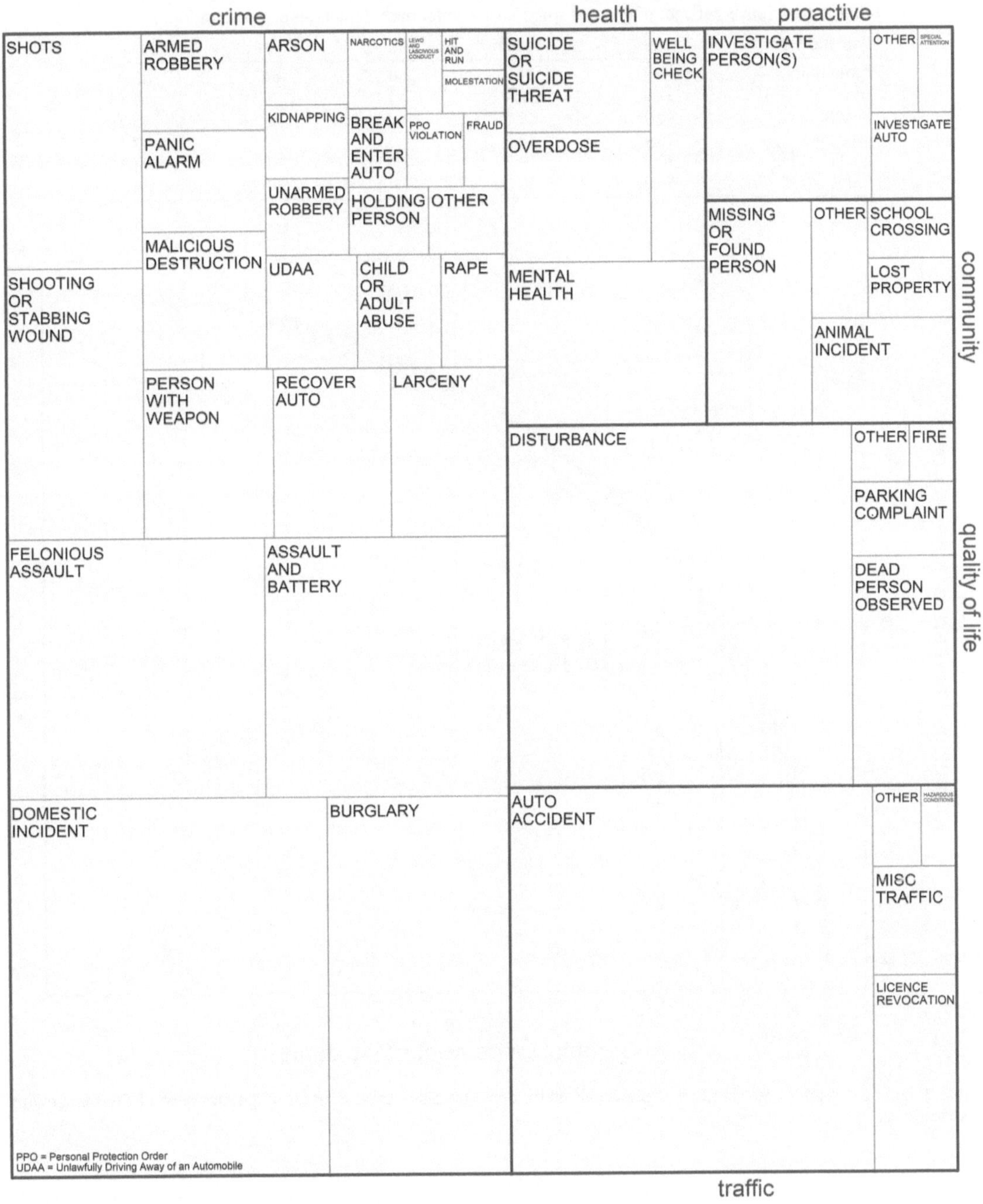

Figure 1. Proportional breakdown of police time consumed over the year, defined as time spent on the scene, for each call category.

5.3 Spatio-temporal patterning

Mean incident counts by day of the week and by hour of day, for each demand classification, are visualized in Figure 3. This demonstrates that the different types of public demand for police services, as indicated by the six demand classifications, can have a distinct temporal patterning. Community calls appear to concentrate on weekdays, around lunchtime, when other classes of

Table 2. Descriptive statistics of minutes spent on scene for each demand-type classification.

Demand type	Mean	Median	Min.	Max.	SD
community	40.0	24.6	0.1	847.7	48.0
crime	51.0	30.4	0.1	987.0	64.1
health	40.9	29.1	0.1	897.4	45.2
proactive	28.4	16.5	0.1	907.9	47.4
quality of life	30.5	19.7	0.1	885.6	41.1
traffic	55.0	30.0	0.1	901.1	65.0

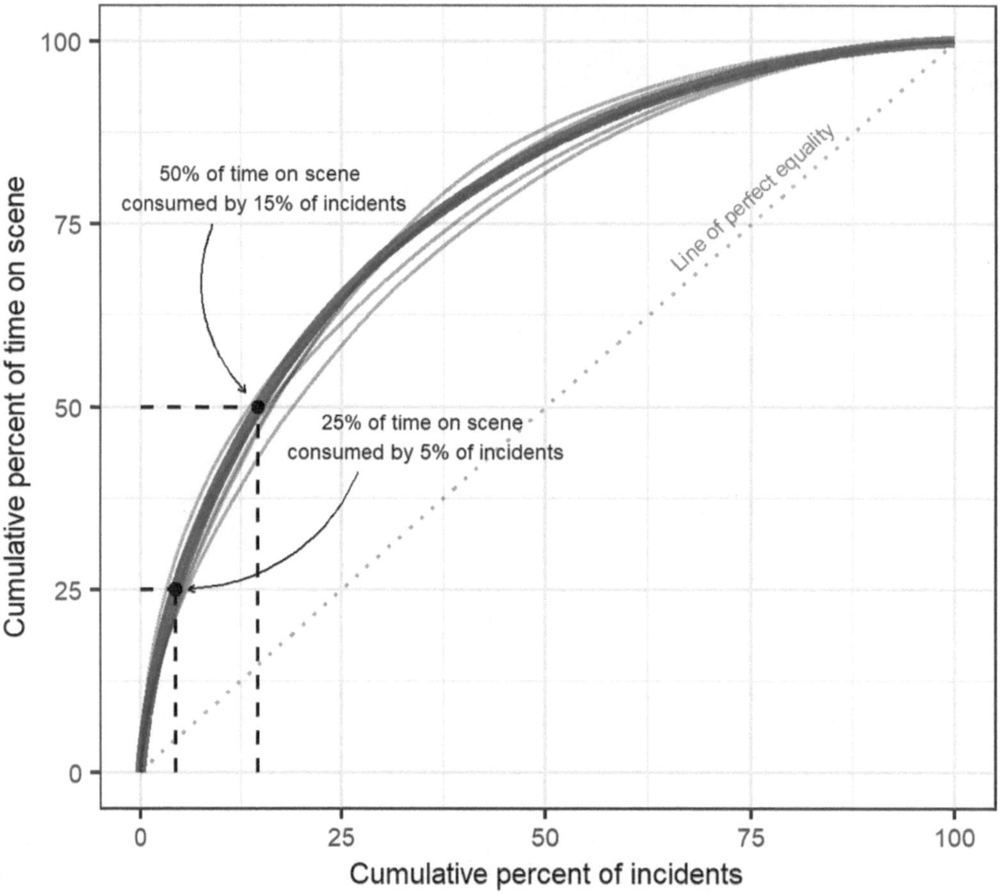

Figure 2. Lorenz curve for time spent on scene across all incidents (in blue). Lorenz curves in grey for each of the six demand classifications.

demand are low. Crime and quality of life-related calls both appear to occur in the evening and early hours of the morning. Traffic incidents concentrate in the evenings, particularly on a Friday. Proactive policing does not have a distinct hourly patterning, but this could be attributed to the low hourly counts. Calls relating to health issues, the primary interest of Ratcliffe (2021), appear to largely take place in the evening and early morning.

The spatial patterning of police demand in Detroit, defined as the aggregate time spent on the scene throughout the year, is visualized for each demand classification in Figure 4.[5] This demonstrates that the time police spent attending to incidents is highly concentrated in space and can vary between different demand types. The police spend a considerable amount of time around the Wayne State University (WSU) and Midtown attending to community, proactive and quality of life

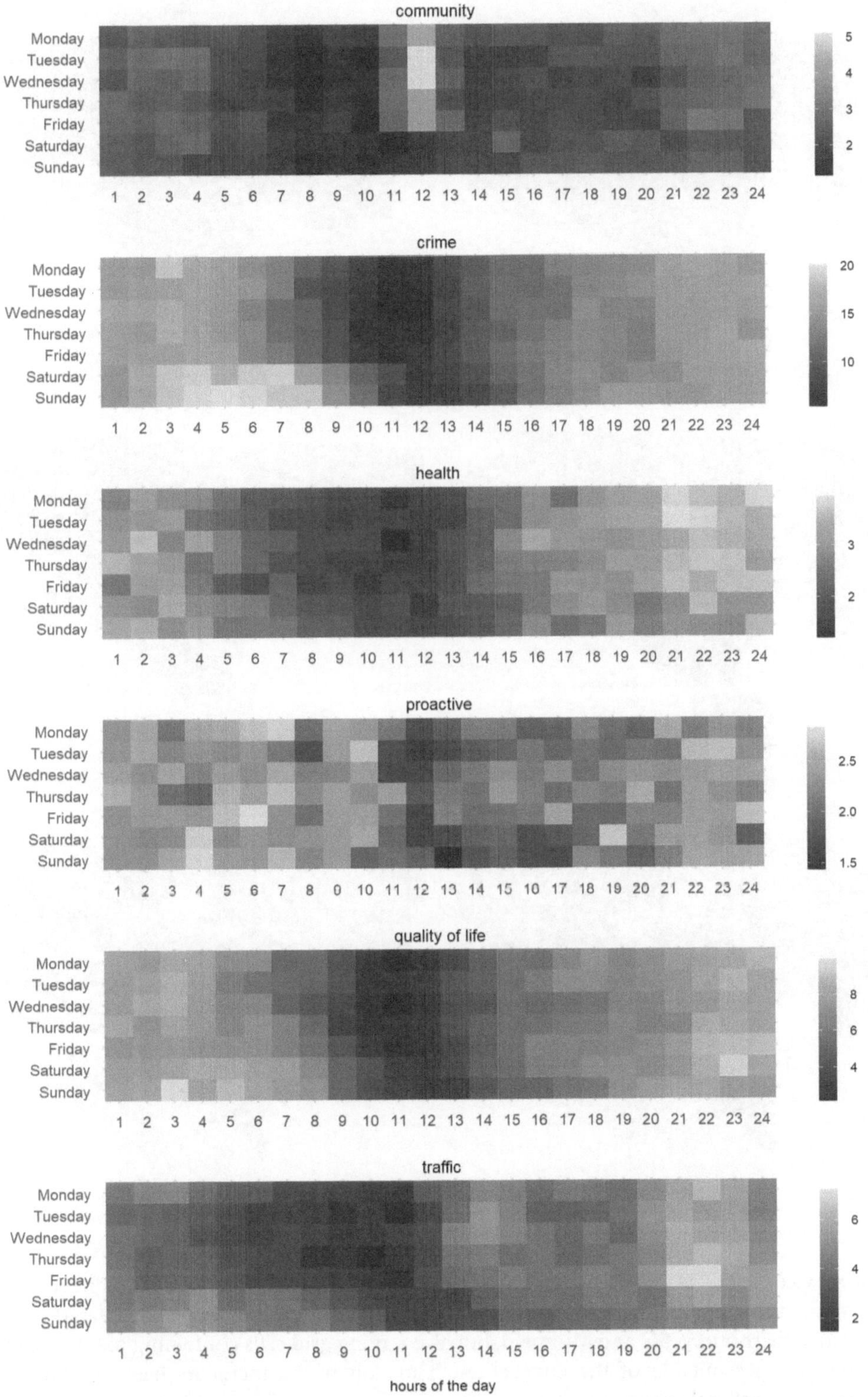

Figure 3. Mean call counts by day and hour, for each demand type.

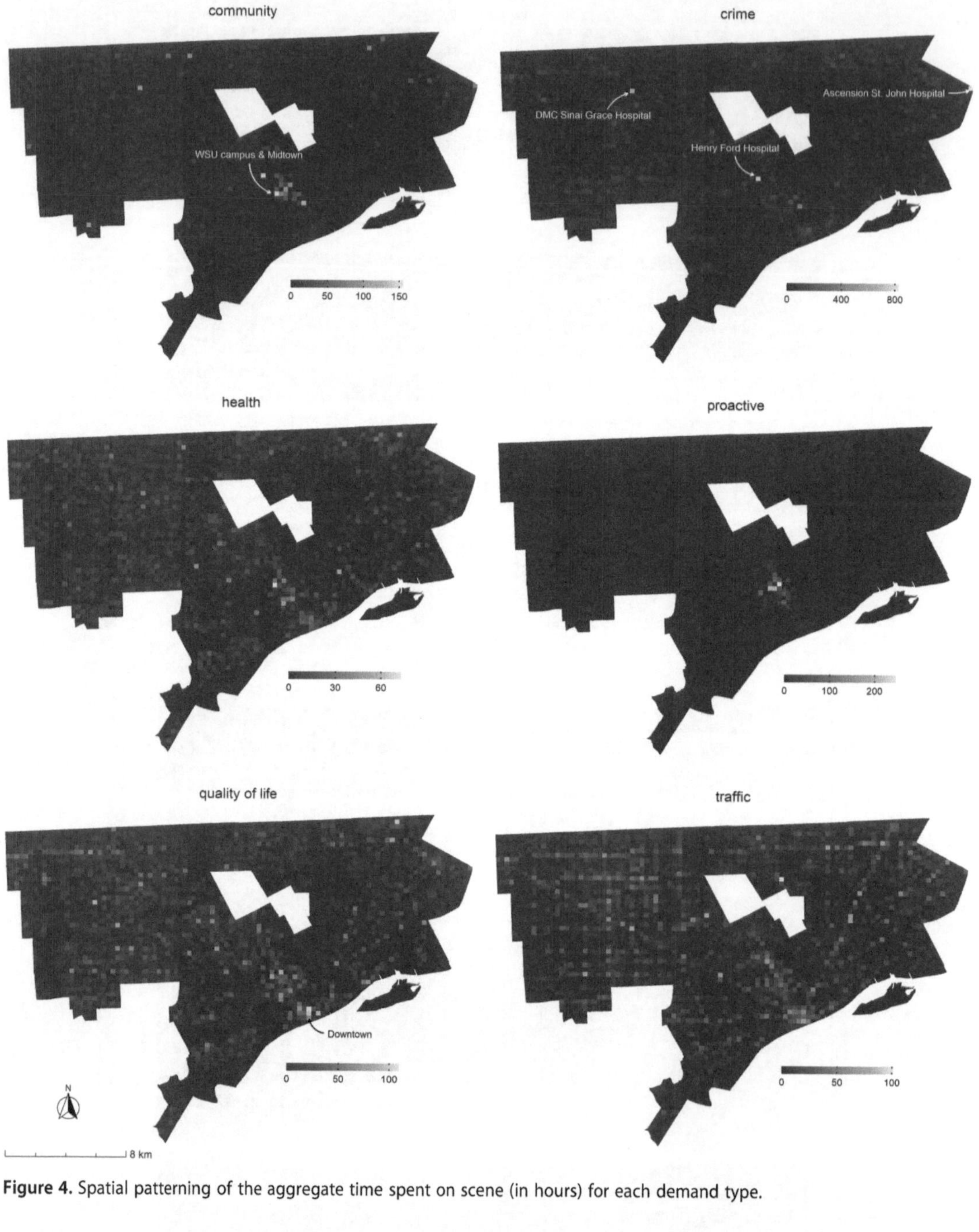

Figure 4. Spatial patterning of the aggregate time spent on scene (in hours) for each demand type.

calls for service. Officers spend vast amounts of time on crime-related calls in or near hospitals, most notably, the Henry Ford Hospital. Police time spent attending to health-related calls concentrates in and around WSU and Midtown, but also among grid cells containing mental health and well-being facilities outside of the city center. Time on traffic incidents has a distinct spatial patterning along arterial roads into Downtown.

6 Discussion

In replication and extension of the main findings reported by Ratcliffe (2021) and Lum et al. (2021), this contribution has described the scale and composition of calls for police service in Detroit, US. Broadly speaking, the results presented here provide robustness to those reported by Ratcliffe (2021) and Lum et al. (2021). There is substantial empirical evidence to demonstrate that, in multiple jurisdictions, the public rely on the police for both social *and* crime-fighting functions. The evidence highlights the potential implications of radically reforming police forces in the United States. A reduction in the capacity of the police to meet emergency demand, without first providing appropriate, capable, and accessible replacement emergency services, could have considerable repercussions for public safety and well-being. This contribution provides the first such demonstration using open data and open code, opening up analyses for scrutiny, reuse, and extension by the public, academics, and/or police practitioners. We encourage usage of the materials provided with this study to replicate analyses across other jurisdictions. In doing so, we hope to see a consistent and reliable evidence-base across different contexts for the purposes of comparison and generalization.

In this study, calls were categorized according to the six classes used by Ratcliffe (2021). The overall composition of police demand in terms of call volume and proportional time spent is remarkably similar. A considerable volume of calls for service, and in turn, a considerable proportion of deployed police time, relate to incident types which do not fall under the traditional 'crime-fighting' role of the police. Instead, the police fulfill a variety of other social service functions, including the resolution of public (mental) health incidents and resolving community issues. That said, descriptive statistics which drill down into the underlying distribution of officer time consumed by each demand type provide additional insight which would otherwise be overlooked. First, it is clear that there is considerable variation in the amount of time consumed both between and within demand classifications. On a methodological point, this shows how average (e.g., mean times) or aggregate (e.g., sum times) measures might mask the underlying variation. Second, and relatedly, these extensions demonstrate that a disproportionately large amount of police time is spent on a small number of emergency calls. Fifty percent of total time on scene in consumed by just 15% of calls. High-demand calls will likely be complex and/or life-threatening incidents or calls which require officers to secure a scene for extended periods of time. A targeted examination of these calls might shed light on the extent to which such high-intensity demands could be reduced or better resolved through or in concert with other public services.

In this regard, this study raises useful discussion points around the different measures of officer time. First, it is clear that findings on the scale and composition of police demand are only marginally sensitive to whether measures of officer time include the response time – defined as the time from dispatch to when the first officer arrives on-scene. The overall findings are almost identical between the two measures. Here, we would highlight that our response time measure did not include dispatch time, but rather, travel time in isolation. Including dispatch time would increase the gap between the two measures: low-priority calls will be held in the dispatch queue for longer, inflating the overall response time, while high-priority calls will be dispatched rapidly. Since certain calls will have higher priority responses (e.g., violent crime), this gap is likely to differ between demand classifications. We excluded dispatch time on the basis that it does not capture deployment, but a specific investigation into its impact would be straightforward using the open materials provided.

Second, and relatedly, we would reiterate that the 'time on scene' measure reported here, in alignment with Lum et al. (2021), refers to the amount of time which elapses between when the first officer arrives and when the last unit clears the scene. This differs from that of Ratcliffe (2021) which accounted for the number of officers attending the scene. Lum et al. (2021) note that including backup officers in the time calculation might introduce complications. For instance, non-serious incidents might receive backup unnecessarily, particularly during periods of low-demand, which would inflate the time consumed and overstate the resources required to resolve such an incident. Although the overall composition of police demand is comparable between Philadelphia (Ratcliffe, 2021) and Detroit, the true impact of these measures remains unclear. We propose that future research investigate these distinctions. This would require CAD (or equivalent) data, timestamped at each stage of the response (dispatch, scene arrival, scene departure), for individual police units nested within calls. This level of granularity would permit the calculation and comparison of multiple measures of officer time, as well as an investigation into the extent to which backups and/or 'flocking' might influence such measures. In sum, further investigations into different measures of 'police time' and the corresponding impact on our assessment of the scale and composition of police demand are necessary before we can claim that the evidence-base is sufficient.

The spatial and temporal patterning of demand for police services in Detroit demonstrates that different demands often originate from different places and can concentrate during different times of the day. Given the specialized training and experience required to deal with certain forms of police demand (e.g., well-being checks, suicide threats), forces might consider accounting for this variation when assigning personnel to shifts and patrol areas, or organizing co-patrols with other social services. We would emphasize that space-time hotspot policing and co-responder initiatives should be tailored for specific demand types, including disaggregated crime types. Pilot studies are already underway in this area, including the policing of mental health issues within hotspots characterized by violence and drug crimes (White & Weisburd, 2018). This is supported by recent research which has shown that, at least in the Canadian context, mental-health-related calls for service can have a different spatial patterning to crime (Vaughan et al., 2016) but that there is considerable overlap when it comes to violence (Hodgkinson & Andresen, 2019). The co-dependence of specific criminal and non-criminal forms of demand in time and space would support moves to deepen collaboration between different social services, rather than bringing about a radical shift in supply away from the police in isolation.

The spatio-temporal findings presented here might prompt further investigations into the underlying environmental factors generating different forms of police demand. Recent research has found that the explanatory frameworks underpinning environmental criminology (e.g., place attractors) are relevant for non-criminal forms of demand, such as those calls involving emotionally disturbed persons (Vaughan et al., 2016). That said, we know little about the nuances of how different environmental characteristics might drive different forms of demand in the same study area. The study materials made available here could be extended using open data resources, such as Open Street Map, to provide a theoretically driven investigation into the urban character (e.g., place attractors) of high-demand areas according to the six demand classifications. Based on the distinct temporal patterning of different demand types, such analyses should be time-sensitive, capturing, for instance, the ambient population flows of different places throughout the day, or the opening times of risky facilities. To date, ambient population analyses have focused on crime-specific calls for service (Andresen & Brantingham, 2007) which, as we have seen, constitute only part of the emergency demands placed on police. These advancements would move analyses beyond descriptive accounts of specific study regions to a generalizable causal model of police demand.

The study is not without shortcomings. First, while the Detroit data permit an open and reproducible case site, the raw incident data do not make a distinction between the initial call classification and the final disposition. This would permit a comparison, as conducted by Ratcliffe (2021), into the extent to which the call handler's initial incident classification changes following the attendance of officers at the scene. Here, we cannot conduct such an investigation. Second, findings presented here, and those reported by Ratcliffe (2021) and Lum et al. (2021), rely on the reliability and validity of police incident classifications. These are imperfect. Recent evidence from the United Kingdom and Canada indicates that police under-record the proportion of emergency calls involving persons with mental ill-health, which in turn underestimates the amount of police time consumed by such incidents (Koziarski et al., 2022; Langton et al., 2021). Investigations into recording practices and call handler decision-making will be necessary to further understand this issue across US police jurisdictions (see, Lum et al., 2020; Simpson, 2021).

Notes

1. Accessible via https://data.detroitmi.gov/.
2. In the raw data, the time between dispatch and first on-scene arrival is referred to as *travel time*. The *intake* and *dispatch time* are reported; however, we did not consider these measures to reflect deployment time. We return to this point in the discussion.
3. We refer readers to the corresponding GitHub repository for further details on how call descriptions were combined (https://github.com/langtonhugh/demand_detroit). Readers unfamiliar with R code can review the reference table entitled 'categorization summary'.
4. The purpose of the graphic is to provide a broad summary, in replication of Ratcliffe's visual. The numbers underlying the graphic are reported in the corresponding GitHub repository.
5. Noting that the aggregate time spent on scene may be influenced by outliers, the raw count maps and underlying distributions are reported in the Appendix. These indicate that 'high time' outliers do not seriously misrepresent the aggregate figures in Figure 4.

Disclosure statement

No potential conflict of interest was reported by the author(s).

Funding

This research was carried out within the What Works in Policing research programme of the NSCR and funded by the Netherlands Police.

ORCID

Samuel Langton http://orcid.org/0000-0002-1322-1553
Stijn Ruiter http://orcid.org/0000-0003-2872-2710
Tim Verlaan http://orcid.org/0000-0002-3048-5817

References

Andresen, M. A., & Brantingham, P. J. (2007). *Hot spots of crime in Vancouver and their relationship with population characteristics*. Ottawa: Department of Justice Canada.

Bennell, C., & Blaskovits, B. (2019). The case for open police research. In R. Mitchell & L. Huey (Eds.), *Evidence based policing: An introduction* (pp. 117–131). Policy Press, University of Bristol.

Bernasco, W., & Steenbeek, W. (2017). More places than crimes: Implications for evaluating the law of crime concentration at place. *Journal of Quantitative Criminology*, *33*(3), 451–467. https://doi.org/10.1007/s10940-016-9324-7

Boulton, L., McManus, M., Metcalfe, L., Brian, D., & Dawson, I. (2017). Calls for police service: Understanding the demand profile and the UK police response. *The Police Journal*, *90*(1), 70–85. https://doi.org/10.1177/0032258X16671032

Ellison, M., Bannister, J., Lee, W. D., & Haleem, M. S. (2021). Understanding policing demand and deployment through the lens of the city and with the application of big data. *Urban Studies*, *58*(15), 3157–3175. https://doi.org/10.1177/2F0042098020981007

Hodgkinson, T., & Andresen, M. A. (2019). Understanding the spatial patterns of police activity and mental health in a Canadian city. *Journal of Contemporary Criminal Justice*, *35*(2), 221–240. https://doi.org/10.1177/1043986219842014

Huey, L., & Bennell, C. (2017). Replication and reproduction in Canadian policing research: A note. *Canadian Journal of Criminology and Criminal Justice*, *59*(1), 123–138. https://doi.org/10.3138/cjccj.2016.E09

Koziarski, J., Ferguson, L., & Huey, L. (2022). Shedding light on the dark figure of police mental health calls for service. *Policing: A Journal of Policy and Practice*. https://doi.org/10.1093/police/paac006

Langton, S., Bannister, J., Ellison, M., Haleem, M. S., & Krzemieniewska-Nandwani, K. (2021). Policing and mental ill-health: Using big data to assess the scale and severity of, and the frontline resources committed to, mental ill-health-related calls-for-service. *Policing: A Journal of Policy and Practice*, *15*(3), 1963–1976. https://doi.org/10.1093/police/paab035

Lum, C., Koper, C. S., Stoltz, M., Goodier, M., Johnson, W., Prince, H., & Wu, X. (2020). Constrained gatekeepers of the criminal justice footprint: A systematic social observation study of 9-1-1 calltakers and dispatchers. *Justice Quarterly*, *37*(7), 1176–1198. https://doi.org/10.1080/07418825.2020.1834604

Lum, C., Koper, C. S., & Wu, X. (2021). Can we really defund the police? A nine-agency study of police response to calls for service. *Police Quarterly*, July. https://doi.org/10.1177/2F10986111211035002

Lum, C., & Koper, C. S. (2021). Guest post: Shifting mental health calls away from police will not greatly affect their workload. *The Washington Post online*. https://www.washingtonpost.com/dc-md-va/2021/08/30/guest-post-911-analysis/

McNeeley, S., & Warner, J. J. (2015). Replication in criminology: A necessary practice. *European Journal of Criminology*, *12*(5), 581–597. https://doi.org/10.1177/1477370815578197

Ratcliffe, J. H. (2021). Policing and public health calls for service in Philadelphia. *Crime Science*, *10*(1), 1–6. https://doi.org/10.1186/s40163-021-00141-0

Simpson, R. (2021). Calling the police: Dispatchers as important interpreters and manufacturers of calls for service data. *Policing: A Journal of Policy and Practice*, *15*(2), 1537–1545. https://doi.org/10.1093/police/paaa040

van Dijk, A., & Crofts, N. (2017). Law enforcement and public health as an emerging field. *Policing and Society*, *27*(3), 261–275. https://doi.org/10.1080/10439463.2016.1219735

Vaughan, A. D., Hewitt, A. N., Andresen, M. A., & Brantingham, P. L. (2016). Exploring the role of the environmental context in the spatial distribution of calls-for-service associated with emotionally disturbed persons. *Policing: A Journal of Policy and Practice*, *10*(2), 121–133. https://doi.org/10.1093/police/pav040

White, C., & Weisburd, D. (2018). A co-responder model for policing mental health problems at crime hot spots: Findings from a pilot project. *Policing: A Journal of Policy and Practice*, *12*(2), 194–209. https://doi.org/10.1093/police/pax010

Wood, J. D., Watson, A. C., & Barber, C. (2021). What can we expect of police in the face of deficient mental health systems? Qualitative insights from Chicago police officers. *Journal of Psychiatric and Mental Health Nursing*, *28*(1), 28–42. https://doi.org/10.1111/jpm.12691

1. Appendix

1.1. Raw count maps

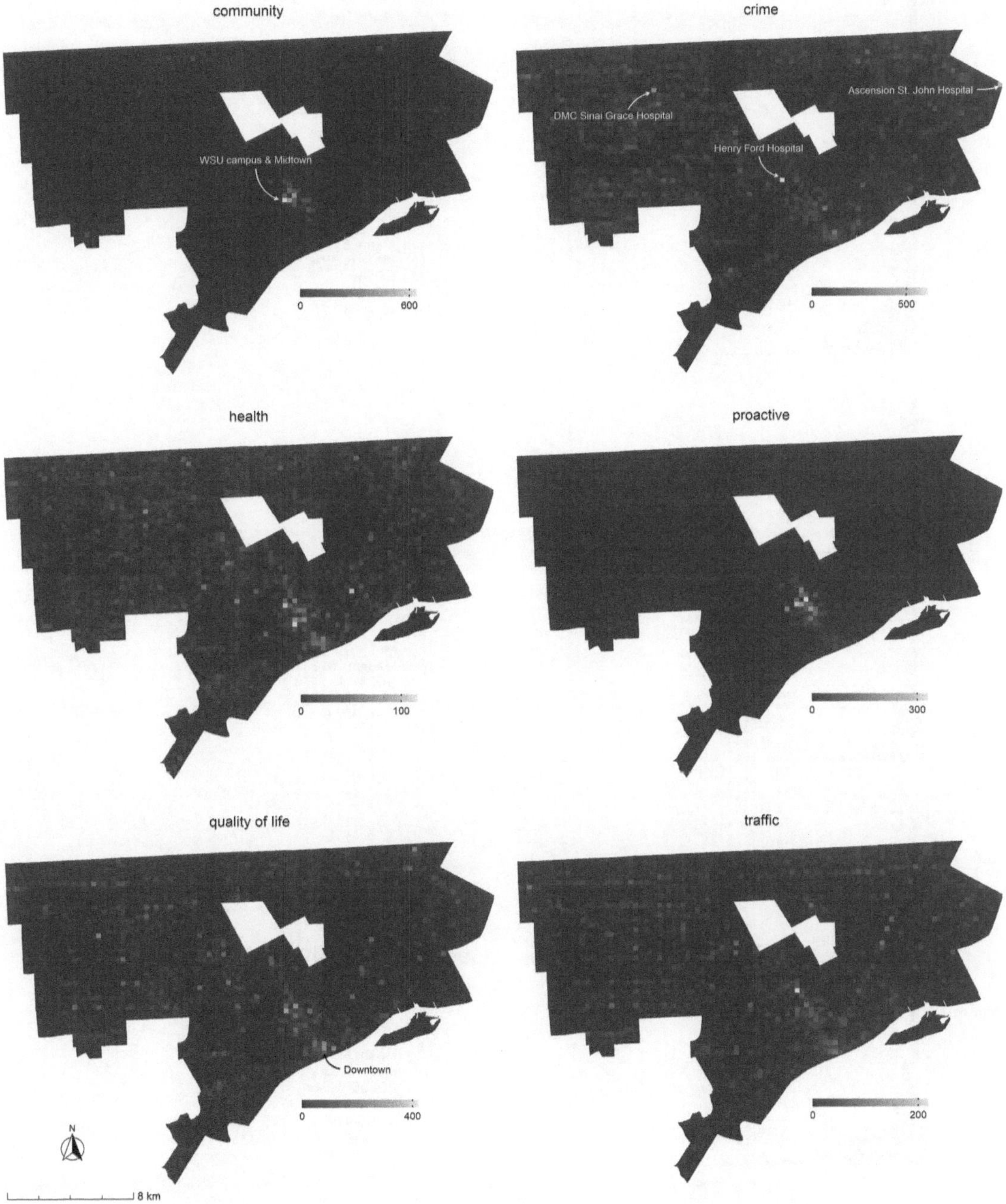

Figure 5. Spatial patterning of the raw call counts for each demand classification.

1.2. Time on scene distributions

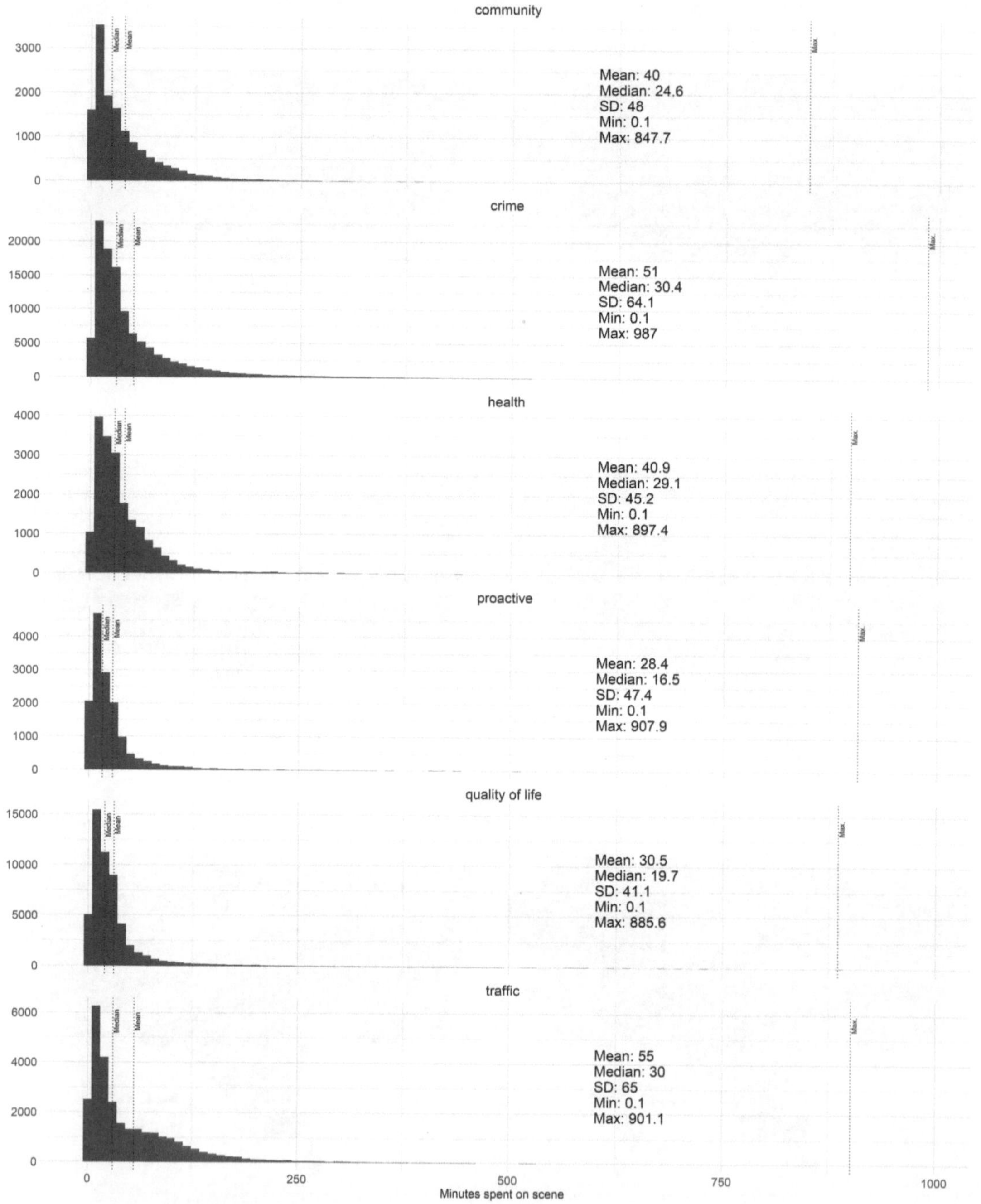

Figure 6. Distribution and descriptive statistics of time spent on scene by demand classification at the call level.

A street segment analysis of crime in a township: evidence from South Africa

Kayla Theron, Gregory Dennis Breetzke, Lourens Snyman and Ian Edelstein

ABSTRACT

Street segments as a micro-level unit of analysis have become increasingly popular in spatial crime research with a plethora of studies having shown how crime spatially concentrates at this spatial scale. The vast majority of this research has, however, emanated from the United States and other 'Westernized' cities, with little attention on less developed contexts. Developing countries have different structural and design conditions from developed countries and this could be reflected in micro-spatial crime patterns. In this study, we undertook the first street segment analysis of crime in southern Africa with a particular focus on the township of Khayelitsha, located approximately 30 kilometers from Cape Town. Townships are uniquely South African urban settlements, borne out of repressive apartheid-era spatial planning policies. Results showed that violent, property, and sexual crimes concentrate spatially in Khayelitsha at the street segment level with substantial street-to-street variability. From a practical perspective, so-called 'hot streets' should be the primary focus of intervention by law enforcement agencies tasked with reducing crime in countries with far less resources than their Global North counterparts. We recommend replication of this analysis in other African contexts in order to build up a body of evidence to either support or challenge the notion of 'crime concentration at micro-places' commonly advocated by international scholars.

Introduction

It is well-known that place greatly influences criminal behaviour with a range of studies finding the concentration of crime in space across almost all continents (Andresen, 2006; Brantingham & Brantingham, 1995; Breetzke, 2018; Curman et al., 2015; Favarin, 2018; Groff et al., 2010; Wuschke et al., 2021). Historically, researchers examining spatial crime concentrations have done so at coarse levels of aggregation (see, Bursik & Grasmick, 1993; Kubrin & Weitzer, 2003; Sampson & Groves, 1989; Sampson et al., 1997) with the census tract being the most common in the United States, for example. Notwithstanding the inherent methodological problems of using pre-existing census geography in spatial criminology (see, Bailey & Gattrell, 1995; Openshaw, 1984), there is a growing realisation, as outlined by Braga et al. (2017), that larger places, such as neighbourhoods, are spatially heterogenous and may contain dramatically varying micro-environments which pose different risks for crime. Indeed, there are areas within neighbourhoods that may exhibit low, or no crime whatsoever. Consequently, only a particular micro-environment (i.e., street) within a neighbourhood may be responsible for the majority of crime occurring there with a combination of these high crime micro-places causing the larger neighbourhood itself to be perceived as being criminogenic; a problem known as 'averaging' (see, Weisburd et al., 2009). This increased acknowledgement that finer street segments may provide a more accurate, and perhaps nuanced, indication of crime risk has led to a plethora of studies examining crime concentrations at the street segment level of spatial aggregation (Chainey et al., 2019; Favarin, 2018; De Melo et al., 2015; Umar et al., 2021; Weisburd et al., 2012; Weisburd & White, 2019; Wuschke et al., 2021). The vast majority of this research has, however, been undertaken in the developed world, with much less known outside this context. The present study aims to make a small but meaningful contribution in this regard by undertaking the first street segment analysis of crime in southern Africa. Specifically, we conduct a street segment analysis of crime in Khayelitsha, a township located approximately 30 kilometers from the city of Cape Town on the southwestern tip of South Africa.

Literature review

Undertaking a street segment analysis of crime is not new. A large body of work has examined how crime varies spatially at the street segment level (Curman et al., 2015; Favarin, 2018; Groff & Lockwood, 2014; Weisburd & Amram, 2014; Weisburd et al., 2012). The vast majority of this work has found how crime spatially clusters in a relatively few number of streets. One of the first ever 'micro-spatial' studies of crime was undertaken by Sherman et al. (1989) who mapped over 320,000 calls to police in Minneapolis and found that only three percent of addresses accounted for 50% of calls for police. In arguably the most seminal piece of work in this field, Weisburd et al. (2004) found that roughly four percent of street segments in Seattle, Washington, accounted for 50% of crime and, importantly, found that these figures remained relatively constant over a 14-year period (1989–2002). Later, Groff et al. (2010) replicated Weisburd's Seattle study but applied trajectory analysis to find groups of places that follow similar crime trajectories over a 16-year study period. The researchers found a number of instances where individual street segments had trajectories which were unrelated to their immediately adjacent streets indicating some level of inter-street crime variability. Similarly, Braga et al. (2010) examined the spatial stability of robbery at the street segment level in Boston, Massachusetts over a 29-year period and found that almost half of all robberies reported in Boston occurred in roughly eight percent of street blocks. They also found that only 12% of street segments had one robbery incident over the study period. In New York, Herrmann (2012) undertook a spatio-temporal analysis of crime (from 2006 to 2010) and found that the majority of street segments experienced no crime across the five-year study period, further illustrating the disproportionate distribution of crime at the street segment level of analysis. Finally, Hipp and Kim (2016) found that five percent of street segments across 42 cities in southern California accounted for crime at it range from 35% to 100%. Other studies in the US include those of Chalfin et al. (2021), Kim and Hipp (2018), Lee and Eck (2014), and Pierce et al. (1988), and Weisburd et al. (2009), among others.

Studies outside the US have been less forthcoming but include Curman et al. (2015), who found similar spatial trends to those in the US with roughly eight percent of street segments in Vancouver accounting for 50% of crime. These patterns remained stable over time. Also in Vancouver, Andresen et al. (2017) investigated patterns of disaggregated crime types on street segments and found crime to be highly concentrated, regardless of crime type, with most street segment and intersection trajectories being stable over the study period. In Europe, Favarin (2018) undertook a street segment analysis of crime in Milan, Italy, and found four percent and 1.6% of street segments contained 50% of burglaries and robberies, respectively, while in The Hague, Netherlands, Steenbeek and Weisburd (2015) examined over 400,000 police crime records spanning a nine-year period (2001–2009) and found that 50% of all crime incidents occurred on roughly seven percent of street segments in the city. The researchers also compared crime concentrations at the street segment, neighbourhood and district levels and found crime to be more concentrated at the street segment level than at the other spatial levels. Finally, Weisburd and Amram (2014) conducted a street segment analysis of crime in Tel Aviv-Jaffa, Israel and also found substantial crime concentrations with roughly five percent of street segments accounting for 50% of crime. Remarkably, the researchers found that only 0.9% of street segments accounted for 25% of crime, indicating an intense concentration of crime at very particular places throughout the city.

Research articles emanating from outside the developed world are rare but recently a number of studies have emerged that largely support the concentration and stability of crime at this spatial scale. For example, in Campinas, Brazil, De Melo et al. (2015) found that roughly four percent of street segments were responsible for 50% of crime and that roughly 29% of street segments accounted for 100% of crime in the city. A more recent study by Chainey et al. (2019) examined the spatial concentration of crime across 37 cities in South America and found that between 0.8% and 2.5% of street segments accounted for 25% and 50% of crime respectively, across all cities. In Jaipur, India, Mazeika and Kumar (2017) found four hotspots of crime, representing less than one percent of the total land in the study area, accounted for about 23% of burglary incidents while in Turkey, Duru (2010) examined the relationship between high schools, on-premise alcohol outlets, and coffeehouses, and crime on street blocks and found that as the number of these 'target places' increased on a street block, so too did the number of crimes. Importantly, the strength of this relationship varied by the type of place (i.e., strongest in on-premise alcohol outlets and weakest in high schools) and the type of crime, and was also moderated by neighbourhood social disorganisation. We are aware of only one study that has been undertaken in Africa thus far and that was done by Umar et al. (2021) who undertook a street segment analysis of crime in Kaduna, Nigeria. Using crime victimization survey data, the researchers examined the concentration of breaking-and-entering and domestic theft at the street segment level and found that roughly 11% of all street segments accounted for 50% of the two crime types. The results of this collective research provide further evidence for the 'law of crime concentration at place' espoused by Weisburd (2015) which suggests that certain percentage of places accounts for a fixed percentage of crime (e.g., 5% of street segments accounts for 50% of crime across different cities).

From a policing perspective, the increased awareness that crime concentrates spatially has informed a number of crime prevention strategies, notably hotspot policing. The rationale behind hot spot policing – which is aligned with the emergence of the broader intelligence-led policing paradigm (Weisburd & Telep, 2014) – is that directing a variety of police-led crime control efforts towards areas abundant with crime (e.g., particularly a neighbourhood or street segment) will have a disproportionate effect on reducing crime outcomes. The strategy almost always involves the use of crime mapping techniques to first identify micro-places that have a disproportionate amount of crime (Braga et al., 2014) and then assigning appropriate operational and/or tactical resources to these places. A common (and early) critique of place-based policing interventions such as hot spots policing is that crime will simply displace to surrounding areas (e.g., Reppetto, 1976). While there is some evidence of crime displacement across a city (Hodgkinson et al., 2020), increasing evidence suggests that areas around targeted hotspots are more likely to be associated with the diffusion of crime control benefits than crime displacement (Bowers et al., 2011; Clarke & Weisburd, 1994; Weisburd et al., 2006).

The vast majority of studies evaluating the impact of hotspot policing on reducing crime outcomes has been undertaken in the United States (see, Ariel & Partridge, 2016; Braga & Bond, 2008; Kochel et al., 2015; Taylor et al., 2011; Uchida & Swatt, 2013, among others) with researchers overwhelmingly finding that this prevention strategy works, to varying extents. Studies outside the United States are less numerous but have largely reinforced these findings. For example, in the United Kingdom (UK), Bland et al. (2021) found that adopting this strategy resulted in an up to 40% reduction in criminal incidents in 21 high-crime neighbourhoods in Bedfordshire, while Williams (2015) found similar reductions in crime in the West Midlands but also found that fewer policing units of longer duration in hot spot areas were associated with a greater reduction in crime, than more frequent shorter patrols. Interestingly, Sherman (2022) examined how hot spots policing has been used as a common law enforcement strategy in the UK and found that the strategy is moving away from traditional ad-hoc approaches *across* policing institutions towards building an evidence-base that uses continuous impact assessment *within* policing agencies and the hot-spots themselves. Other evaluations have occurred in Denmark (Attermann, 2017), Sweden (Marklund & Merenius, 2014), Columbia (Blattman et al., 2017), and Uruguay (Chainey et al., 2021) with statistically significant effect sizes most often found favouring the effects of hot spots policing in reducing crime outcomes at treatment places. Finally, a systematic review and meta-analysis of 65 studies containing 78 tests of hot spots policing interventions by Braga et al. (2019) found robust evidence that hot spots policing reduces crime outcomes and does not appear to result in the spatial displacement of crime into areas immediately surrounding targeted locations.

Notably absent in all this work, however, are studies emanating from Africa in general, and southern Africa, in particular, which is a shortcoming of existing research, since African cities possess vastly different urban spatialities and street network patterns in comparison to their Global North counterparts. South African cities, and their townships in particular, have unique spatial morphologies which can largely be attributed to its apartheid-era politically-charged urban planning practices with associated implications for policing (see, Faull, 2016). Cities in Africa are also growing at an alarming rate. Indeed, according to Bearak et al. (2021) thirteen of the world's 20 biggest urban areas will be in Africa by the end of the century – up from just two in 2021 – as will more than a third of the world's population. Crime in Africa is also a major socioeconomic problem caused, at least historically, by the uneven distribution of wealth and power, and a labour surplus (Kibuka, 1980) but increasingly attributed to an increase in organized crime activity (Global Organized Crime Index, 2021). Further evidence of micro-spatial crime concentrations at this spatial level in Africa will add a measure of academic credibility and generalizability to past research that has examined this phenomenon.

The study area

Khayelitsha is a township located on the urban periphery of Cape Town. In South Africa, a 'township' refers to a built-up residential area on the periphery of former Whites-only urban areas. Under the apartheid policy focusing on separate development, these areas were originally reserved for non-White people only (i.e., Black African, Coloured and Indian population groups) although townships are still predominantly (>95,0%) inhabited by non-Whites. When they were established during the 1950s and 1960s they were never intended to grow into fully developed and independent communities with a complete infrastructure (e.g., shops, schools, community and recreational facilities, work places). They were seen as largely dormitory towns for mainly male migrant workers from the then 'Bantustans' or homelands.[1] Currently, most townships still include a more stable, higher socio-economic (chiefly lower middle class) area inhabited by people who have lived there for a long period of time or whose parents/relatives had lived there since the establishment of the township. These older and more established areas may have developed features such as taverns, clubs, recreational facilities and churches, which have turned such areas into fully fledged communities although most often still lacking in basic infrastructure and services. However, around or next to such areas more informal settlements and 'matchbox' developments that have sprang up since democracy. Although not intended, these differ little from the original dormitory towns. Writing about townships under apartheid, Chikane (1986) described them as typically characterized by widespread malnutrition, poor or non-existent health systems, ill-equipped and overcrowded schools, inadequate or non-existent social security, and high levels of unemployment.

Khayelitsha is the largest township in the Western Cape province of the country with a population of roughly 400,000 inhabitants, of which almost 99% are black African. It is one of last townships that was 'created' in apartheid South Africa in 1983 by the former apartheid government. The township was intended to house predominantly Xhosa-speaking black Africans and concomitantly provide a cheap form of migrant labour for the then former Whites-only neighbourhoods located in the central business district and surrounding neighbourhoods of Cape Town. Despite the arrival of democracy in 1994, Khayelitsha remains poor and socially and economically marginalised from Cape Town. Roughly 40% of residents of Khayelitsha are unemployed, with youth unemployment (aged 15–23) at over 50% (Statistics South Africa, 2011).[2] Approximately 74% of households have a monthly income of R3,200 or less (~US$200). Notably, crime is of particular concern in Khayelitsha with the main policing precinct consistently among the most violent precincts in the country with contact crime[3] in particular almost double the national average (Crime Hub, 2021). Despite its high levels of crime, recent research in Khayelitsha has, however, shown how crime spatially concentrates in a relatively few number of neighbourhoods (see, Breetzke & Edelstein, 2019) providing some initial local evidence of the 'law of crime concentration at places', albeit at an aggregate level. It is however, not yet known whether this spatial concentration of crime is amplified or more diffuse at the finer street segment level of analysis.

Data and methods

Crime data

The crime data used in this research study was obtained from the South African Police Service (SAPS).[4] These data contain information pertaining to the location, and date and time of occurrence of crime committed in the Khayelitsha policing precinct over a five-year period: 2012–2016.[5] Included in the crime data were unique identifiers for each crime, an x and y geo-coordinate, and the type of criminal offence recorded. From this dataset, a separate sexual (rape, attempted rape, sexual assault, and indecent assault), violent (murder, attempted murder, and common assault) and property (house, bank, and business robbery,[6] as well as common robbery with or without firearms) crime type was extracted in order to determine the extent to which the concentration of crime at the street segment level of analysis is uniform across crimes with varying motives and operandi. Khayelitsha experienced a total of 3,942 violent crime, 3,017 property crime and 666 sexual crime incidents during the five-year research period (total = 7625). Importantly, we do not aim here to specifically unpack reasons *why* certain categories of crime may nor may not concentrate at the street segment level, rather the intention of this descriptive paper is to determine *if* crimes cluster at the street segment level in this unique context and provide some preliminary explanations for what we find.

It is important to note at this juncture that perhaps the biggest limitation of this study relates to the reliability and accuracy of the crime data we used. Crime is notoriously under-reported in Khayelitsha (see, O'Regan et al., 2014) where residents have simply lost faith in the police to maintain law and order. Moreover, the geospatial accuracy of crime data in the country has also been brought into question (see, Edelstein & Arnott, 2019). Faced with these challenges, spatial crime researchers in South Africa have two choices. Either undertake research with the only official and spatially replete crime dataset available, whilst acknowledging the limitations, or seek alternative ways of getting 'proxy' crime data. We choose the former option, knowing that what we find may not be the exact magnitude and location of crime occurring during this study period in Khayelitsha but being relatively certain that the data we have broadly approximates its true magnitude and distribution. Previous researchers have speculated on how to undertake spatial crime research using alternative crime data sources both locally (see, Faull, 2019) and internationally (Gray et al., 2017). However, these options (such as the use of casualty/trauma, and emergency medical services data) were not available to us for this research. As an aside, it should be noted that the under-reporting of crime is not a uniquely South African problem (see, Jaitman & Anauati, 2020), neither is the under-reporting of crime necessarily 'worse' in more deprived regions of cities or countries when compared to more affluent areas. Recently, Buil-Gil et al. (2021) found that the 'dark figure' of crime in geographic areas in the United Kingdom for example, is larger not only in areas that are deprived but *also* in wealthy areas, dispelling the notion of the under-reporting of crime being synonymous with crime in less developed contexts. Their research confirmed previous findings in the US from Baumer (2002) who showed that citizens living in more deprived neighbourhoods, as well as those living in wealthy areas, are less likely to inform the police of a criminal incident.

Street centreline data

A dataset representing the street centreline for the City of Cape Town was obtained from the City of Cape Town Open Data Portal.[7] This data consisted of line features that were segmented at every road intersection and were represented as the two block faces on both sides of a street between two intersections. There were 107,466 segments in the dataset with each segment containing a number of attributes including the road name, surface type, speed limit (in kilometres per hour) and segment length in metres, among others. Of this network, streets within the Khayelitsha policing precinct were extracted which resulted in a total of 1,400 street segments with an average segment length of roughly 112 metres, and a standard deviation of approximately 180 metres. The shortest length was just a few metres while the longest street segment was over 12 kilometres long. Given the high variability of street segment lengths we next decided to split the street segments into 50 metre 'lengths', while preserving street segments already split at intersections. This also resulted in some variability in street segment length as street segments did not obviously nest within 50 metre increments across intersections but the variability in length was significantly reduced and the median and modal street segment lengths were both 50 metres. We believe that this 'normalisation' provides a more accurate representation of crime at this spatial level since longer streets will necessarily contain more crime due to their increased length. Whilst we could have normalised the data by the length of the street (for example, crimes per metre) we felt that, from a policing perspective, knowing which sub-segments of a street contained more crime provided better information for law enforcement agents. The final study area street network had 3,253 street segments.

Analysis

Following Weisburd and Amram (2014) and others, we converted a crime point's location to a street segment using the Spatial Join tool in ArcPro. This resulted in a dataset representing crime incidents with corresponding segment identifiers. Note that crime incidents were only associated with one corresponding street segment, not multiple street segments (i.e., a single crime incident was only spatially associated to the nearest street segment ensuring that segments did not share the same crime incidents). Simple crime counts per 50 metre street segment were then calculated and mapped. We are aware that crime counts represent the discrete number of crime events, rather than estimates or ratios, and are greatly dependent on the crime data itself, which is vulnerable to under- and over-reporting. We decided, however, at this initial stage, to use counts to display the trends descriptively. Future research could aim to use more advanced geospatial techniques to further tease out the trends we find here.

Results

On average, there were 2.3 crime incidents per street segment across all crime types during the study period with the most crime-prone street segment experiencing 119 crime incidents in total. There were more violent crimes per street, followed by property crimes and sexual crimes, with violent crime also being the most dispersed throughout the study area. Roughly 37% of street segments (1,219 out of 3,253) in Khayelitsha did not experience any crime during the five-year study period. Violent crime was recorded in 49% (1,579) of street segments, while property crime was recorded in

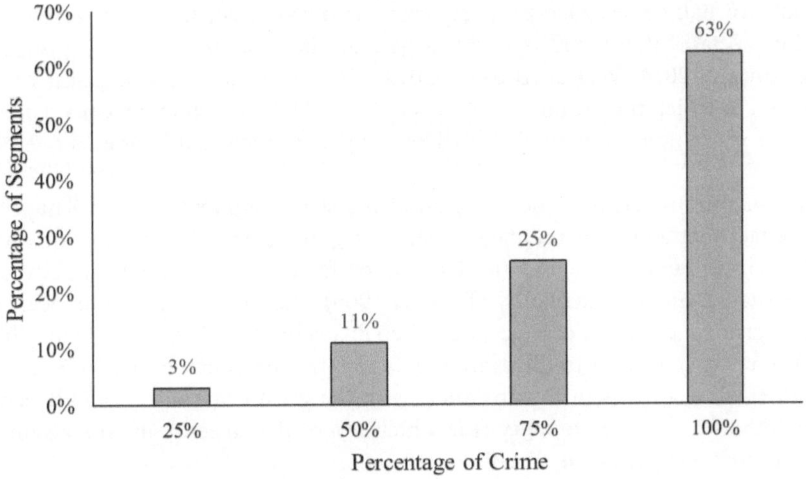

Figure 1. Percentage of street segments that account for 25%, 50%, 75%, and 100% for all crime.

42% (1,378) of street segments and sexual crime in 14% (454) of street segments, respectively. This preliminary analysis shows that despite its reputation for crime (see, Breetzke & Edelstein, 2019), almost two-thirds of streets in Khayelitsha precinct experience no crime.

Figure 1 shows the percentage of street segments that account for various percentages of all crime in Khayelitsha. The results presented here are similar to past research which has most often found high concentrations of crime in a relatively small number of streets. Indeed, previous research has shown that between two and six percent of streets produce roughly half of all crime (see, De Melo et al., 2015; Weisburd & Amram, 2014; Weisburd et al., 2004). Our results are more dispersed with 11% of streets producing half of all crime, but just three percent of street segments in the precinct containing 25% of all crime. Figure 2 shows the same percentages but for the three different crime types. Again, similar trends emerge with a low percentage of street segments accounting for a large percentage of crime, across all types. Violent crime is the most dispersed crime type followed by property crime and sexual crime. Even so, just 327 street segments in Khayelitsha were responsible for half of all violent crime occurrences while 272 street segments

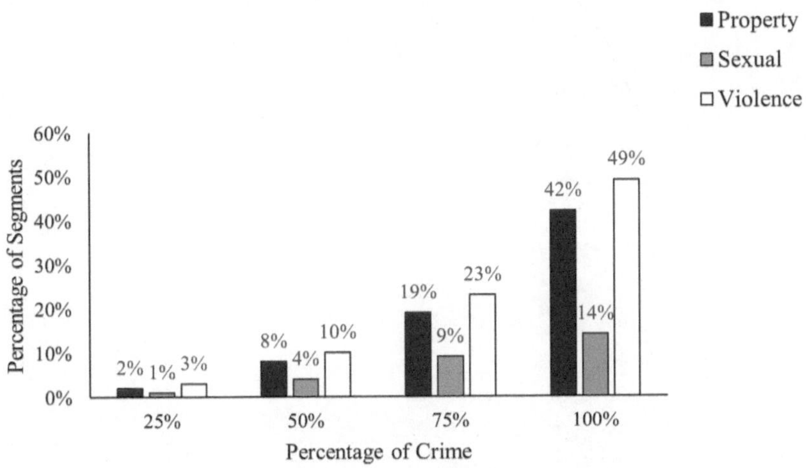

Figure 2. Percentage of street segments that account for 25%, 50%, 75%, and 100% of violent, property and sexual crime respectively.

were responsible for half of recorded property crime and 454 street segments were responsible for *all* sexual crime. Again, these findings are largely similar to the results of previous research (Weisburd & Amram, 2014; Weisburd et al., 2012). However, one notable point of difference is the varying extent to which the number of streets in Khayelitsha precinct have no crime. In the case of sexual crime, for example, roughly 86% of streets have no recorded incidents over the five-year study period.

To further illustrate the crime concentration at the street segment level in Khayelitsha and to account for the fact that a large percentage of street segments experience no crime, we calculated variants of the Lorenz curve as well as the Gini index for each crime type. Initially developed to measure and visualize income inequality (Lorenz, 1905), the Lorenz curve has been increasingly used to examine crime concentrations (see, Bernasco & Steenbeek, 2017; Umar et al., 2021). In these studies, the Lorenz curve is used to illustrate the cumulative proportion of crime occurring across spatial units, or street segments in this instance, with the greater the distance between the Lorenz curve and the line of maximum equality (for which x% of the street segments account for y% of crime), the more unequal the crime distribution.

While the Lorenz curve is an effective way to visualize inequity in crime distributions, the Gini index (Gini, 1912) highlights overall inequity of its distribution. After Umar et al. (2021), the index is the ratio (A/B) of the area of the chart between the expected line of equality and the observed distribution (i.e., A), and the area of the chart above the expected line of equality (i.e., B – A is a subset of B). The index ranges from zero which indicates that the distribution of crime across street segments is entirely equal, while a value of 1 indicates the distribution of crime is completely unequal, suggesting that all crime incidents occur in only one street segment. Analysis was done using the R package, 'lorenzgini', which was uniquely designed by Bernasco and Steenbeek (2017) for sparse crime data across small units of analysis (i.e., the generalized version). Specifically, when there are more spatial units than crime events (i.e., many street segments with no crime) as was the case in this study.

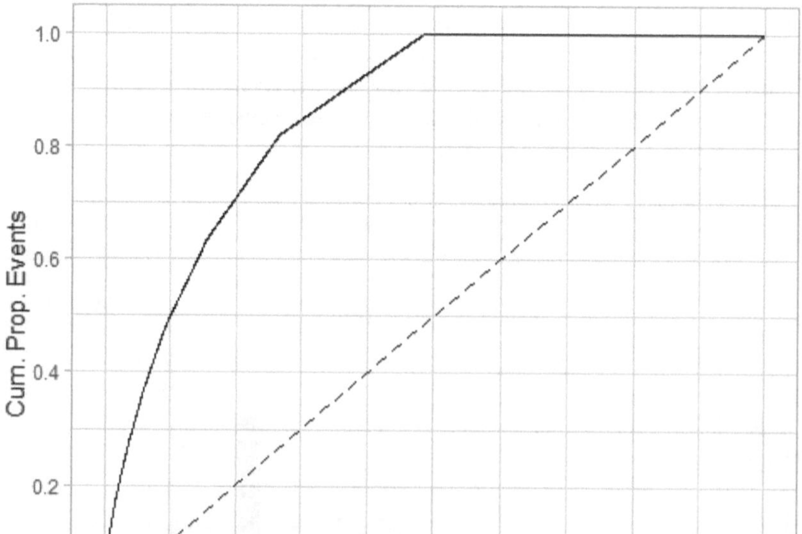

Figure 3. Cumulative concentration curve for violent crime.

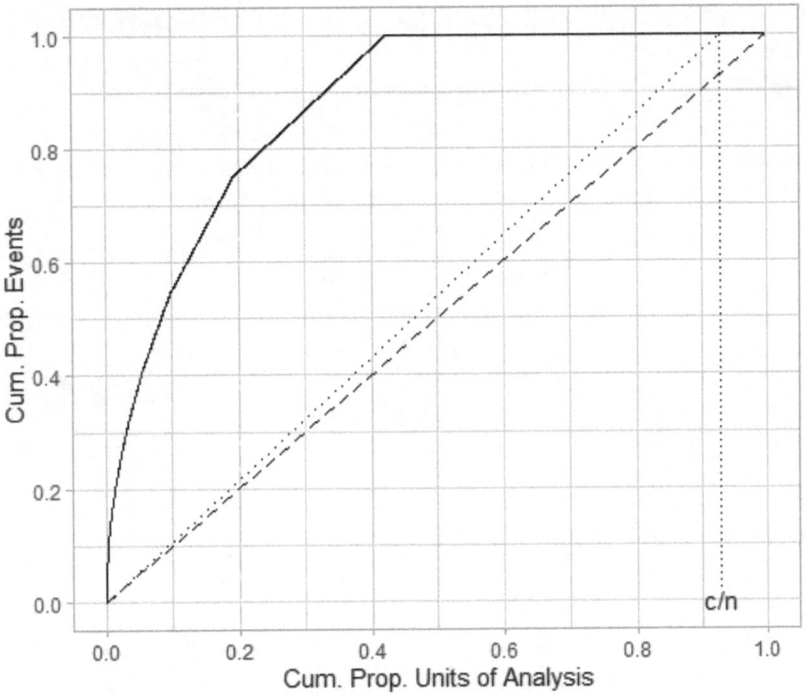

Figure 4. Cumulative concentration curve for property crime.

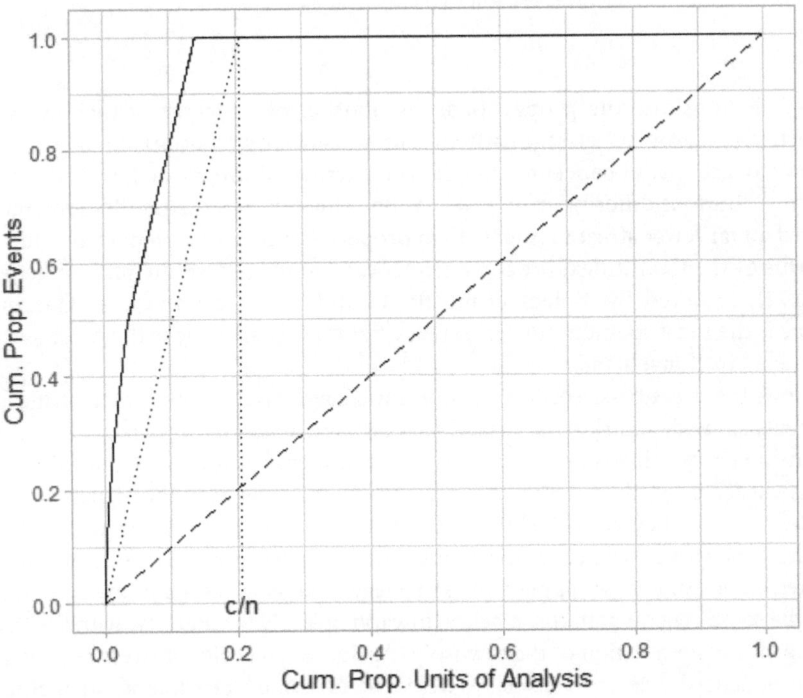

Figure 5. Cumulative concentration curve for sexual crime.

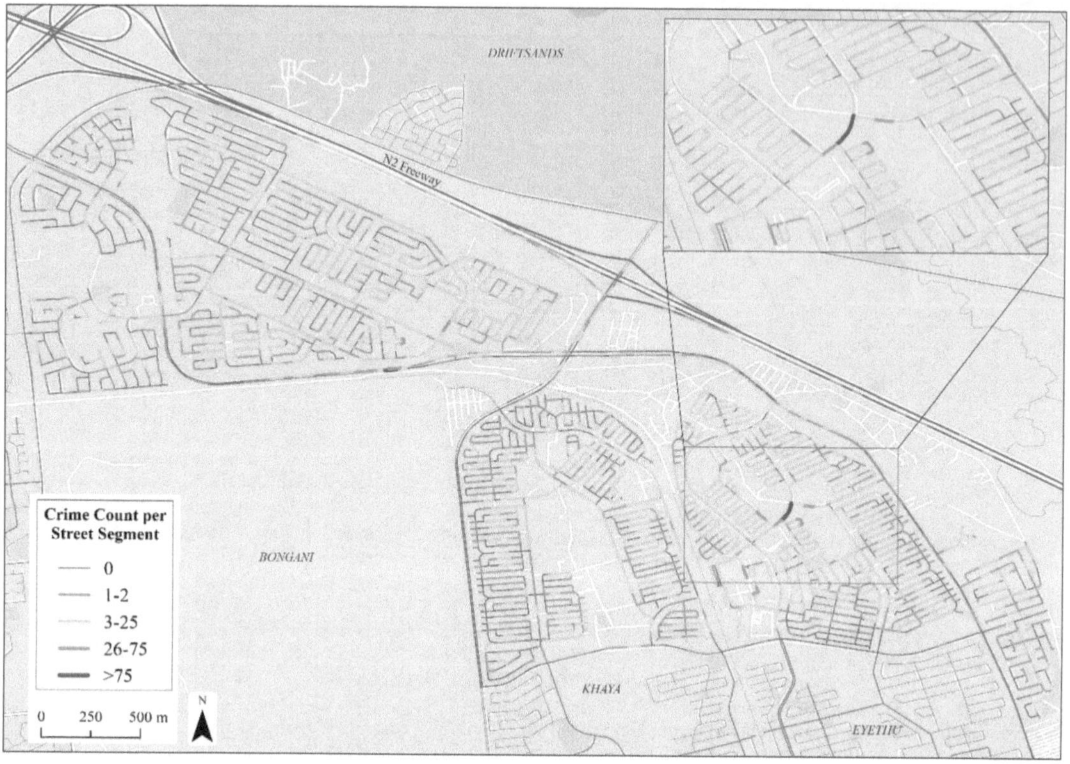

Figure 6. Distribution of all crime at the street segment level in Khayelitsha.

Figures 3–5 demonstrate the proportional distribution of property, sexual and violent crime events, respectively, across street segments in Khayelitsha using Lorenz curves. All figures once again demonstrate the spatial concentration of crime across all three categories with the curves for the observed distributions differing from expectation. These curves further demonstrate that sexual crime occurred on far fewer street segments than property crime and violent crime during the study period. In terms of the Gini Index, property crime was found to have the highest generalized Gini coefficient (0.73), followed by violent crime (0.71) and sexual crime (0.5). This indicates that property crime is the most spatially concentrated, whereas sexual crime is the most dispersed across all street segments in Khayelitsha.

Figure 6 shows the street-by-street crime counts for Khayelitsha. It is noticeable that a large number of street segments along the outskirts of Khayelitsha contained little to no crime (1–2 incidents). Street segments with moderate crime (3–25 incidents) were scattered throughout the township, but were predominantly clustered together. A total of three street segments were in the highest crime streets (>75 incidents) category, and they collectively accounted for roughly four percent of all crime recorded. Figures 7–9 show the street-by-street crime counts for Khayelitsha precinct by crime type. In order to make the patterns comparable, we applied the same legend classes to each crime type. All three crime types exhibit the same general patterns, albeit with varying levels of intensity, with the 'hottest' streets located in the south-eastern region of the township. Again, the majority of street segments throughout the township experienced little or no crime, regardless of the crime type while substantial street-to-street crime variability exists with low crime street segments often being adjacent to higher crime street segments.

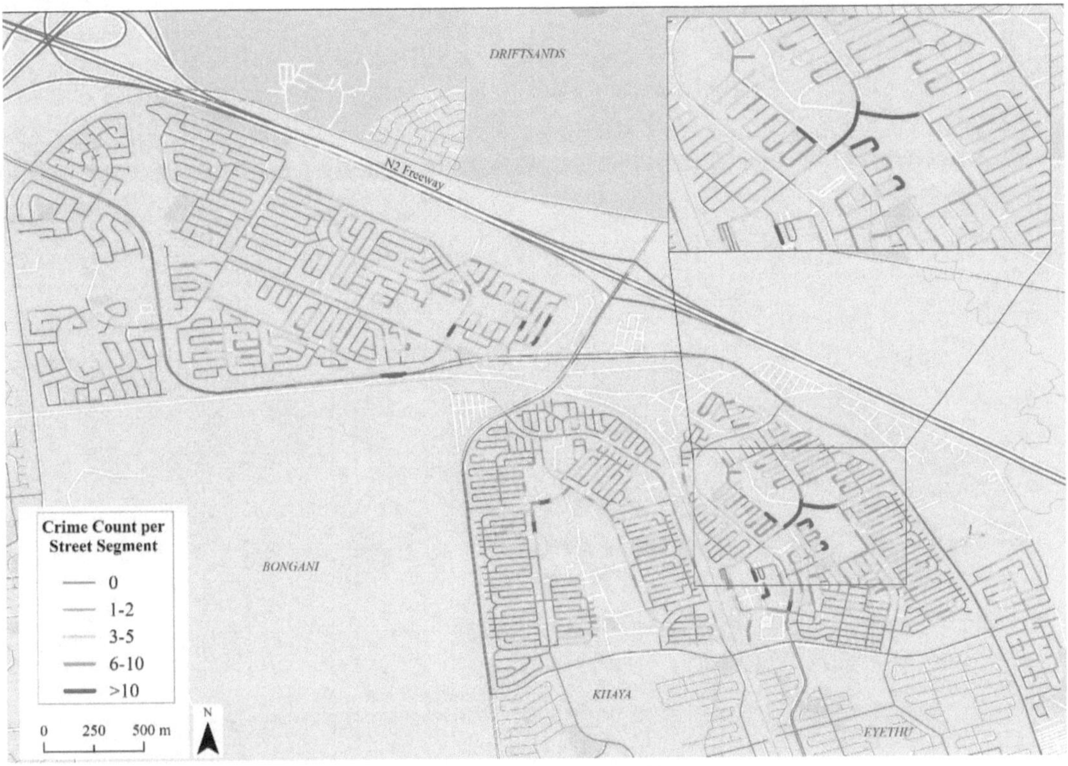

Figure 7. Distribution of violent crime at the street segment level in Khayelitsha.

Discussion

The results of this study are consistent with previous research that has found clear spatial concentrations of crime at the street spatial scale (see, Braga et al., 2010; Herrmann, 2012; De Melo et al., 2015; Weisburd et al., 2004). All crime, as well as crime across the three individual categories, were all found to be spatially concentrated in a relatively few number of streets. The most concentrated crime type was sexual crime, followed by property crime, and violent crime. A number of factors may account for these trends, with the most prevalent being that these spatial concentrations simply reflect broader criminogenic processes (encompassing the built environment, social, economic and other factors) that are playing out at the street segment level in Khayelitsha. Indeed, Umar et al. (2021) argue that the spatial concentration of crime at the street segment level may simply reflect nothing more than the distribution of crime opportunity at this spatial scale. Opportunities in this instance may be residential properties (for property crime) and/or other facilities in the built environment, such as alcohol outlets or schools (which have both been found to be spatially associated with crime, both locally (Breetzke et al., 2021; Matzopoulos et al., 2020), and internationally (Pridemore & Grubesic, 2013)). In their research, Umar et al. used variations of the Lorenz curve and the Gini index to show how crime concentrated in Kaduna, Nigeria at the street segment level beyond the spatial distribution of crime 'opportunity'. Other studies using similar methods include Steenbeek and Weisburd (2015), Johnson and Bowers (2010), and Davies and Johnson (2015). In our study, we did not 'control' for crime opportunities, per se, but rather, in a way similar to Weisburd's and Amram (2014) study in Israel, provide a simple test for the 'law of concentrations of crime at place' proposition in a new and unique location. Future research could examine whether these concentrations intensify or dissipate after accounting for

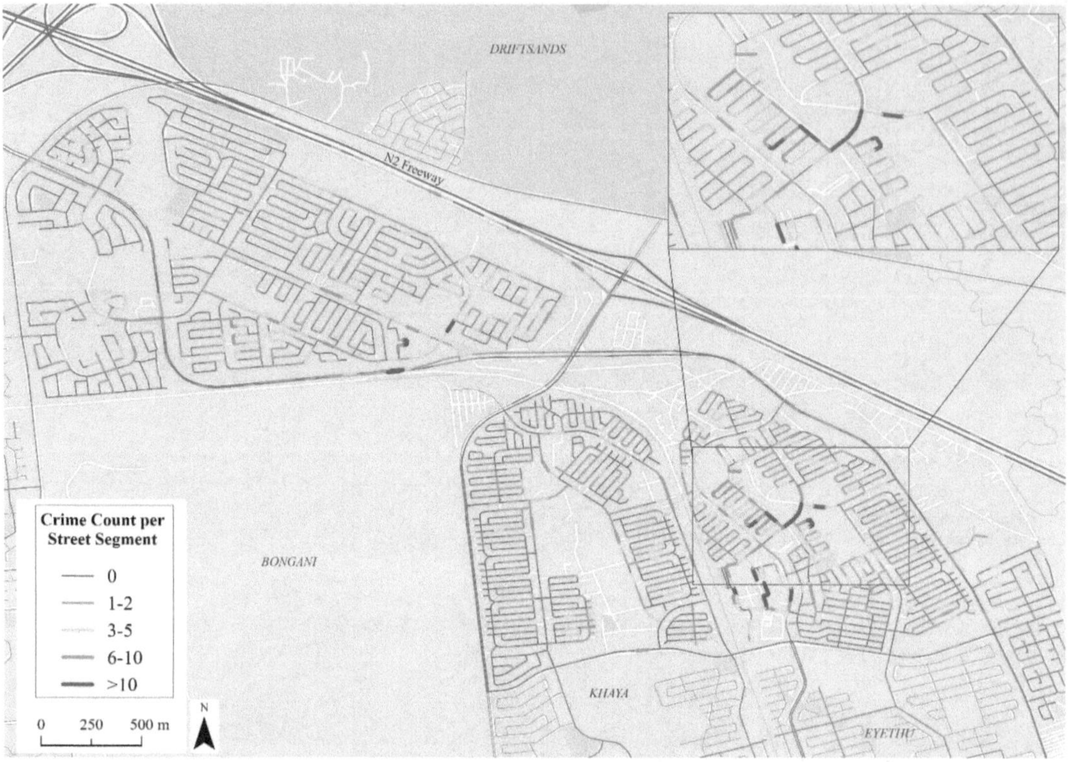

Figure 8. Distribution of property crime at the street segment level in Khayelitsha.

expectation, although it should be noted that identifying crime opportunities in Khayelitsha is challenging. This is largely due to the informal nature of the township where just over one half of all dwellings are shacks (Statistics South Africa, 2011), with limited to no formal street address. In terms of population, official statistics state the size of the township at just under 400,000 (Statistics South Africa, 2011) but unofficial figures of up to 1.2 million have been noted (Cronje, 2014), making risk based on population size or density prone to error. The township is also notoriously under-developed with relatively few formal built facilities. In fact, the first shopping mall in the township was only constructed in 2005; this for an area similar in population size to Atlanta (in the US) or Liverpool (in the UK). These combined factors make more comprehensive future micro-spatial research incorporating the underlying environmental backcloth harder to undertake, but the challenges are not unsolvable and certainly present an avenue for future research.

Importantly, the results of the research provide further evidence for the law of crime concentration at place in South Africa although at a much finer spatial scale than has previously been found in the country. In earlier work, Breetzke and Edelstein (2019) found crime at the coarser sub-place level in Khayelitsha to be spatially concentrated and temporally stable however these trends could mask sub-area spatial heterogeneity, as discussed earlier. Here we found greater spatial concentrations of crime at the finer street segment level of analysis. In her review of 44 empirical studies examining crime concentration at place, Lee et al. (2017) found that as the size of the spatial unit declines (from area to street segment and so forth), crime becomes more concentrated; this was found to be the case in a number of different countries. Here, for the first time, we have found the same evidence in South Africa with important associated implications for policing in Khayelitsha. Policing in the township has been described as 'haphazard' with police driven by gut-feel rather than crime intelligence (see, O'Regan et al., 2014). The lack of competence by law enforcement agencies in the township led to the establishment of a formal Commission of Inquiry into policing

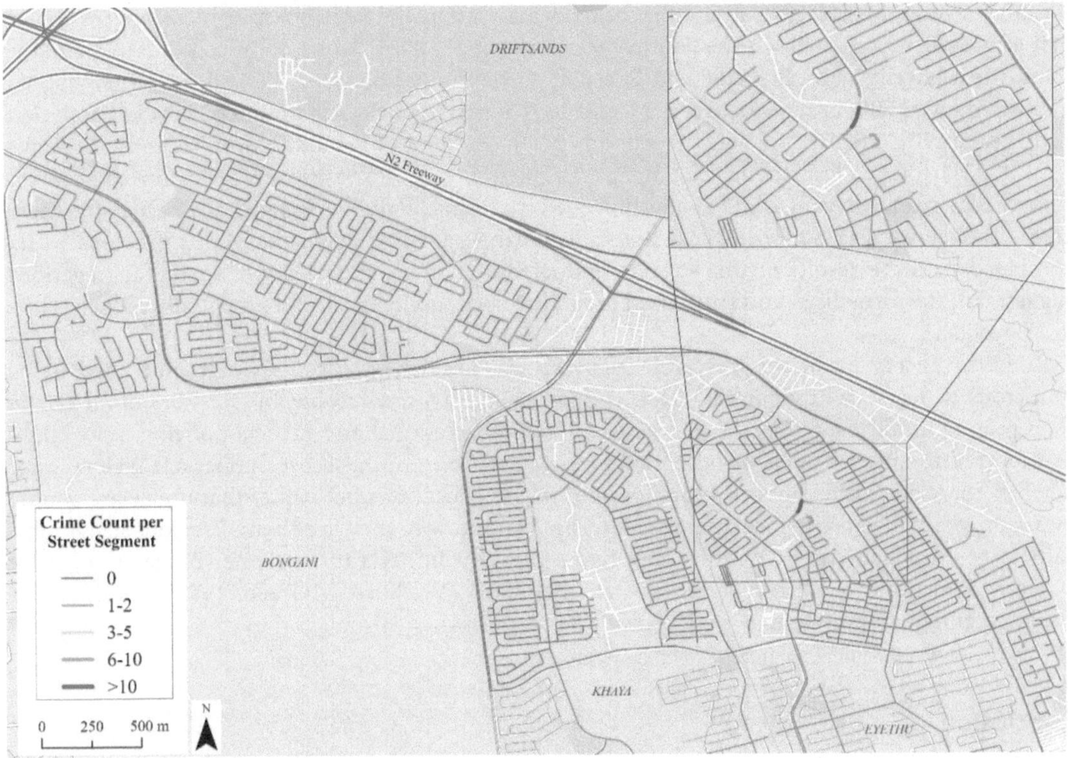

Figure 9. Distribution of sexual crime at the street segment level in Khayelitsha.

in the township in 2012. The Commission was appointed to investigate allegations of police inefficiency in the township, as well as the breakdown in relations between the local community and the police. The results of the Commission were a series of recommendations (outlined in O'Regan et al., 2014) including the need to improve the three key crime intelligence functions including crime mapping, linkage analysis, and on-the-ground intelligence gathering. Crime mapping, in particular, is seen as a mechanism through which more effective policing can be undertaken in the future by highlighting areas of concern. Sadly, none of the proposed recommendations of the Commission's report have been fully implemented (Stoltz, 2021), resulting in crime continuing to be a concern in the township.

The implications of this study from a policing perspective in South Africa are clear. Maximise the scant policing resources available by adopting a hot spots crime prevention strategy in Khayelitsha. In truth a similar type of 'saturation' policing strategy has been sporadically employed by the SAPS over the past decade in certain high-risk neighbourhoods throughout the country. This has most often involved the large-scale deployment of police in high risk areas. The strategy has, however, had limited success with the main issues being its unsustainability, given the limited resources of the SAPS, coupled with the inability of other government departments to deliver developmental interventions at the necessary scale in identified high crime areas (Lamb, 2018). Another form of hot spots 'policing' intervention was implemented in Khayelitsha specifically in July 2019 when the South African National Defence Force (SANDF) was deployed in response to growing gang violence and endemic insecurity. The military intervention was directed at known gang crime hotspots and result in a decrease in crime in affected areas, at least anecdotally (Sullivan, 2020). While the planned intervention was geographically targeted at known hotspots, the military 'occupied' these areas for three months (which was subsequently extended by another six months), rather than conduct periodic patrols (before departing in March 2020). Hot spots policing as a crime prevention strategy has yet to be formally adopted by the SAPS, despite increasing evidence that crime clusters spatially in the country (Breetzke et al., 2021; Horn & Breetzke, 2009). In fact, a study in Khayelitsha by Breetzke and Edelstein (2019) found between 7% and 9% of neighbourhoods produced 50% of rape; between 5% and 12% of neighbourhoods produced 50% of robberies; and between 8% and 16% of neighbourhoods produced 50% of assaults. More recently, Breetzke et al. (2021) found clear spatial and temporal clustering of crime in one township adjacent to Khayelitsha, namely Nyanga, and similarly argued that crime could be dramatically reduced in these areas if police were able to visit these hot spots during patrols. The results of this previous work, combined with the results of this study (conducted at a much finer level of spatial aggregation) suggest that the formalised and structured use of hot spots policing should potentially reduce crime in Khayelitsha.

Indeed, the results of this research suggest that these interventions would not need to be numerous to have an exponential effect. If only 358 streets are responsible for 50% of all crime, then geographically targeting these 'hot streets' with operational and tactical policing units could possibly reduce the risk of crime occurring in these locations. In this sense, it does not really matter whether there are 'crime opportunities' present in these locations but rather that police are simply aware of *where* they are before attempting to understand *why* they are there. Previous geographically-targeted policing interventions have had significant impacts upon crime (Braga et al., 2014; Braga & Weisburd, 2010; Haberman & Ratcliffe, 2015; Weisburd & Green, 1995); South Africa could potentially follow suit.

Conclusion

The main aim of this research was to undertake a street segment analysis of crime in a township. In accomplishing this goal, we believe we have made the following important contributions to the extant literature: First, crime is spatially concentrated at the street segment level in South Africa. While this may be considered a somewhat trivial finding by international spatial crime researchers, the fact that this study is the first of its kind in southern Africa, and only the second in Africa as a whole, makes it a highly significant one. Second, crime is spatially concentrated at the street segment level in a context that is extremely poor – this was also found across all crime types. According to the World Economic Forum (2016), Khayelitsha is one of the five biggest slums in the world with an estimated 32% to 46% of households in the township living in severe poverty. It also has one of the highest rates of violence in the world, outside a conflict zone (Luthy-Kaplan, 2015), with one in three children under 18 likely to become a victim of sexual violence (Inter-Ministerial Committee 2017). This is a context as distant and distinct from the vast majority of cities in the Global North as you are likely to find. Finally, this study is the first in Africa to use official police records to map crime at this spatial scale. While the limitations of using police data have been outlined earlier, it represents the most official dataset available for researchers to undertake this type of replicable research. Future research could potentially utilize other data sources (as outlined by Faull, 2019) to examine micro-spatial crime trends in other contexts in South Africa or across Africa and demonstrate ways in which 'crime opportunities' on streets could potentially influence risk. As a first step, however, we believe that the results presented here, whilst descriptive, are sufficient to merit further investigation and provide an important platform for future micro-spatial crime research in South Africa.

Notes

1. The term 'Bantustan' refers to an apartheid regime policy which set about the creation of 'independent' homelands for black South Africans.

2. This is the most recent census undertaken for which data is available. The 2021 census was postponed due to the Covid-19 pandemic and is in the process of being conducted (July 2022).
3. 'Contact crimes' refer to when a person or people are injured/harmed or threatened with injury/harm during the commission of a crime. A further sub-category of 'contact-related crime' is used for violent crimes committed against property with the intention of causing damage to a person, for example, arson or malicious damage to property.
4. We are unaware of the geocoding accuracy of the crime data provided for us from the South African Police Services (SAPS). Crime data was provided in the form of x and y co-ordinates. The SAPS have previously used GPS devices to record crime in Khayelitsha in areas that are difficult to capture due to a lack of a formal address.
5. The 'Greater Khayelitsha reporting area' consists of three police precincts: Khayelitsha, Harare, and Lingelethu West. We only had access to police data for the Khayelitsha policing precinct. The total population in the Khayelitsha policing precinct is just under 160,000.
6. Robbery is referred to as a property crime in South Africa. It consists of the theft of property by intentionally using violence or threats of violence to induce submission to the taking of it from another.
7. Data downloaded from the City of Cape Town Open Data Portal from https://odp-cctegis.opendata.arcgis.com/datasets/tct-road-centrelines/explore.

Disclosure statement

No potential conflict of interest was reported by the author(s).

ORCID

Gregory Dennis Breetzke http://orcid.org/0000-0002-0324-2254

References

Andresen, M. A. (2006). Crime measures and the spatial analysis of criminal activity. *The British Journal of Criminology*, *46*(2), 258–285. https://doi.org/10.1093/bjc/azi054

Andresen, M. A., Curman, A. S., & Linning, S. J. (2017). The trajectories of crime at places: Understanding the patterns of disaggregated crime types. *Journal of Quantitative Criminology*, *33*(3), 427–449. https://doi.org/10.1007/s10940-016-9301-1

Ariel, B., & Partridge, H. (2016). Predictable policing: Measuring the crime control benefits of hot spots policing at bus stops. *Journal of Quantitative Criminology*, *33*(4), 809–833 1–25. https://doi.org/10.1007/s10940-016-9312-y

Attermann, C. V. (2017). *Investigating hot spots policing*. Ministry of Justice Research Office.

Bailey, T. C., & Gattrell, A. C. (1995). *Interactive spatial data analysis*. Longman.

Baumer, E. (2002). Neighborhood disadvantage and police notification by victims of violence. *Criminology, 40*(3), 579–616. https://doi.org/10.1111/j.1745-9125.2002.tb00967.x

Bearak, M., Moriarty, D., & Ledur, J. (2021). *Africa's rising cities: How Africa will become the center of the world's urban future*. The Washington Post. https://www.washingtonpost.com/world/interactive/2021/africa-cities/

Bernasco, W., & Steenbeek, W. (2017). More places than crimes: Implications for evaluating the law of crime concentration at place. *Journal of Quantitative Criminology, 33*(3), 451–467. https://doi.org/10.1007/s10940-016-9324-7

Bland, M., Leggetter, M., Cestaro, D., & Sebire, J. (2021). Fifteen minutes per day keeps the violence away: A crossover randomised controlled trial on the impact of foot patrols on serious violence in large hot spot areas. *Cambridge Journal of Evidence-Based Policing, 5*(3), 93–118. https://doi.org/10.1007/s41887-021-00066-3

Blattman, C., Green, D., Ortega, D., & Tobón, S. (2017). *Pushing crime around the corner? Estimating experimental impacts of large-scale security interventions*. National Bureau of Economic Research.

Bowers, K., Johnson, S., Guerette, R., Summers, L., & Poynton, S. (2011). Spatial displacement and diffusion of benefits among geographically-focused policing initiatives. *Campbell Systematic Reviews, 7*(1), 1–144. https://doi.org/10.4073/csr.2011.3

Braga, A. A., Andresen, M. A., & Lawton, B. (2017). The law of crime concentration at places: Editors' introduction. *Journal of Quantitative Criminology, 33*(3), 421–426. https://doi.org/10.1007/s10940-017-9342-0

Braga, A. A., & Bond, B. (2008). Policing crime and disorder hot spots: A randomized controlled trial. *Criminology, 46* (3), 577–608. https://doi.org/10.1111/j.1745-9125.2008.00124.x

Braga, A. A., Hureau, D. M., & Papachristos, A. V. (2010). The concentration and stability of gun violence at micro places in Boston, 1980-2008. *Journal of Quantitative Criminology, 26*(1), 33–53. https://doi.org/10.1007/s10940-009-9082-x

Braga, A. A., Papachristos, A. V., & Hureau, D. M. (2014). The effects of hot spots policing on crime: An updated systematic review and meta-analysis. *Justice Quarterly, 31*(4), 633–663. https://doi.org/10.1080/07418825.2012.673632

Braga, A. A., Turchan, B. S., Papachristos, A. V., & Hureau, D. M. (2019). Hot spots policing and crime reduction: An update of an ongoing systematic review and meta-analysis. *Journal of Experimental Criminology, 15*(3), 289–311. https://doi.org/10.1007/s11292-019-09372-3

Braga, A. A., & Weisburd, D. (2010). *Policing problem places: Crime hot spots and effective prevention*. Oxford University Press.

Brantingham, P., & Brantingham, P. (1995). Criminality of place. *European Journal on Criminal Policy and Research, 13*(3), 5–26. https://doi.org/10.1007/BF02242925

Breetzke, G. D. (2018). The concentration of urban crime in space by race: Evidence from South Africa. *Urban Geography, 39*(8), 1195–1220. https://doi.org/10.1080/02723638.2018.1440127

Breetzke, G. D., & Edelstein, I. S. (2019). The spatial concentration of crime in a South African township. *Security Journal, 32*(1), 63–78. https://doi.org/10.1057/s41284-018-0145-2

Breetzke, G. D., Fabris-Rotelli, I., Modiba, J., & Edelstein, I. (2021). The proximity of sexual violence to schools: Evidence from a township in South Africa. *GeoJournal, 86*(2), 765–776. https://doi.org/10.1007/s10708-019-10093-3

Buil-Gil, D., Medina, J., & Shlomo, N. (2021). Measuring the dark figure of crime in geographic areas. small area estimation from the crime survey for England and wales. *British Journal of Criminology, 61*(2), 364–388. https://doi.org/10.1093/bjc/azaa067

Bursik, R. J., & Grasmick, H. (1993). *Neighborhoods and Crime: The dimensions of effective community control*. Lexington Books.

Chainey, S. P., Pezzuchi, G., Guerrero Rojas, N. O., Ramirez, J. L. H., Monteiro, J., & Valdez, E. R. (2019). Crime concentration at micro-places in Latin America. *Crime Science, 8*(5). https://doi.org/10.1186/s40163-019-0100-5

Chainey, S. P., Serrano-Berthet, R., & Veneri, F. (2021). The impact of a hot spot policing program in Montevideo, Uruguay: An evaluation using a quasi-experimental difference-in-difference negative binomial approach. *Police Practice and Research, 22*(5), 1541–1556. https://doi.org/10.1080/15614263.2020.1749619

Chalfin, A., Hansen, B., Lerner, J., & Parker, L. (2021). Reducing crime through environmental design: Evidence from a randomized experiment of street lighting in New York City. *Journal of Quantitative Criminology, 38*(1), 127–157. https://doi.org/10.1007/s10940-020-09490-6

Chikane, F. (1986). Children in turmoil: The effects of unrest on township children. In S. Burman & P. Reynolds (Eds.), *Growing up in a Divided Society* (pp. 333–344). Ravan Press.

Clarke, R. V., & Weisburd, D. (1994). Diffusion of crime control benefits: Observations on the reverse of displacement. *Crime Prevention Studies, 2*, 165–184.

Crime Hub. (2021). *Institute for Security Studies Crime Hub*, https://issafrica.org/crimehub, accessed 2 June 2022

Cronje, J. (2014). *Getting Khayelitsha into perspective*. South Africa: Independent Online. https://www.iol.co.za/news/south-africa/western-cape/getting-khayelitsha-into-perspective-1671699, accessed 2 June 2022

Curman, A. S. N., Andresen, M. A., & Brantingham, P. J. (2015). Crime and place: A longitudinal examination of street segment patterns in Vancouver, BC. *Journal of Quantitative Criminology*, *31*(1), 127–147. https://doi.org/10.1007/s10940-014-9228-3

Davies, T., & Johnson, S. D. (2015). Examining the relationship between road structure and burglary risk via quantitative network analysis. *Journal of Quantitative Criminology*, *31*(3), 481–507. https://doi.org/10.1007/s10940-014-9235-4

de Melo, S. N., Matias, L. F., & Andresen, M. A. (2015). Crime concentrations and similarities in spatial crime patterns in a Brazilian context. *Applied Geography*, *62*, 314–324. https://doi.org/10.1016/j.apgeog.2015.05.012

Duru, H. (2010). *Crime on Turkish streetblocks: An examination of the effects of high- schools, on-premise alcohol outlets, and coffeehouses.* [Unpublished doctoral dissertation]. University of Cincinnati.

Edelstein, I., & Arnott, R. (2019). *Point-level analysis of crime in Khayelitsha: A critical review.* Institute for Security Studies. https://www.africaportal.org/publications/point-level-analysis-crime-khayelitsha-critical-review/, accessed 2 June 2022

Faull, A. (2016). Measured governance? Policing and performance management in South Africa. *Public Administration and Development*, *36*(2), 157–168. https://doi.org/10.1002/pad.1750

Faull, A. (2019). How to map violence without police data. *Institute for Security Studies (ISS) Southern Africa Report*, *22*, 1–24. accessed 2 June 2022 https://issafrica.org/research/southern-africa-report/how-to-map-violence-without-police-data

Favarin, S. (2018). This must be the place (to commit a crime): Testing the law of crime concentration in Milan, Italy. *European Journal of Criminology*, *15*(6), 702–729. https://doi.org/10.1177/1477370818757700

Gini, C. (1912). Variabilità e mutabilita. In E. Pizetti & T. Salvemini (Eds.), *Reprinted (1955) in Memorie di metodologica statistica* (pp. 1–156). Libreria Eredi Virgilio Veschi.

Global Organized Crime Index (2021). *Global initiative against transnational organized crime.* https://ocindex.net/

Gray, B. J., Barton, E. R., Davies, A. R., Long, S. J., Roderick, J., & Bellis, M. A. (2017). A shared data approach more accurately represents the rates and patterns of violence with injury assaults. *Journal of Epidemiology and Community Health*, *71*(12), 1218–1224. https://doi.org/10.1136/jech-2017-209872

Groff, E. R., & Lockwood, B. (2014). Criminogenic facilities and crime across street segments in Philadelphia: Uncovering evidence about the spatial extent of facility influence. *Journal of Research in Crime and Delinquency*, *51*(3), 277–314. https://doi.org/10.1177/0022427813512494

Groff, E. R., Weisburd, D., & Yang, S. M. (2010). Is it important to examine crime trends at a local "micro" level? A longitudinal analysis of street to street variability in crime trajectories. *Journal of Quantitative Criminology*, *26* (1), 7–32. https://doi.org/10.1007/s10940-009-9081-y

Haberman, C. P., & Ratcliffe, J. H. (2015). Testing for temporally differentiated relationships among potentially criminogenic places and census block street robbery counts. *Criminology*, *53*(3), 457–483. https://doi.org/10.1111/1745-9125.12076

Herrmann, C. R. (2012). *Risky businesses: A micro-level spatiotemporal analysis of crime, place, and business establishment type.* [Unpublished doctoral dissertation], City University of New York.

Hipp, J. R., & Kim, Y. A. (2016). Measuring crime concentration across cities of varying sizes: Complications based on the spatial and temporal scale employed. *Journal of Quantitative Criminology*, *33*(3), 595–663. https://doi.org/10.1007/s10940-016-9328-3

Hodgkinson, T., Saville, G., & Andresen, M. A. (2020). The diffusion of detriment: Tracking displacement using a city-wide mixed methods approach. *The British Journal of Criminology*, *60*(1), 198–218. https://doi.org/10.1093/bjc/azz025

Horn, C. A., & Breetzke, G. D. (2009). Informing a crime strategy for the FIFA 2010 world cup: A case study for the Loftus Versfeld stadium in the city of Tshwane, South Africa. *Urban Forum*, *20*(1), 19–32. https://doi.org/10.1007/s12132-009-9054-0

Jaitman, L., & Anauati, V. (2020). The dark figure of crime in Latin America and the Caribbean. *Journal of Economics, Race, and Policy*, *3*(1), 76–95. https://doi.org/10.1007/s41996-019-00042-0

Johnson, S. D., & Bowers, K. J. (2010). Permeability and burglary risk: Are cul-de-sacs safer? *Journal of Quantitative Criminology*, *26*(1), 89–111. https://doi.org/10.1007/s10940-009-9084-8

Kibuka, E. P. (1980). Crime in African countries. *International Review of Criminal Policy*, *35*, 13–23. https://www.ojp.gov/ncjrs/virtual-library/abstracts/crime-african-countries

Kim, Y.-A., & Hipp, J. R. (2018). Physical boundaries and city boundaries: Consequences for crime patterns on street segments? *Crime and Delinquency*, *64*(2), 227–254. https://doi.org/10.1177/0011128716687756

Kochel, T. R., Burruss, G., & Weisburd, D. (2015). *St. Louis County Hot spots in residential areas (SCHIRA) final report: Assessing the effects of hot spots policing strategies on police legitimacy, crime, and collective efficacy.* U.S. Department of Justice.

Kubrin, C. E., & Weitzer, R. (2003). New directions in social disorganization theory. *Journal of Research in Crime and Delinquency*, *40*(4), 374–402. https://doi.org/10.1177/0022427803256238

Lamb, G. (2018). *SAPS stuck in vicious cycle of crackdown policing.* Media24. https://www.news24.com/Columnists/GuestColumn/squeeze-stamp-stabilise-saps-vicious-cycle-of-crackdown-policing-20180611, accessed 25 June 2018

Lee, Y. J., & Eck, J. E. (2014). *Analysis of crime concentration at street segment level.* University of Cincinnati. https://doi.org/10.13140/RG.2.2.17172.91521

Lee, Y.-J., Eck, J. E., O, S., & Martinez, N. N. (2017). How concentrated is crime at places? A systematic review from 1970 to 2015. *Crime Science, 6*(1), 6. https://doi.org/10.1186/s40163-017-0069-x

Lorenz, M. O. (1905). Methods of measuring the concentration of wealth. *Publications of the American Statistical Association, 9*(70), 209–219. https://doi.org/10.2307/2276207

Luthy-Kaplan, K. (2015). *Global health now: An epidemic of child rape in Khayelitsha.* Global Health NOW. https://www.globalhealthnow.org/2015-07/epidemic-child-rape-khayelitsha, accessed 2 June 2022

Marklund, F., & Merenius, S. (2014). *Policing crime "hot spots": Results and experiences from two projects against personal abuse and abuse.* Stockholm: BRÅ. https://www.bra.se/download/18.12caa4f91440b31239f14c0/1394020836016/2014_15_Brottsf%C3%B6rebyggande_polisarbete_i_hot_spots.pdf

Matzopoulos, R., Bloch, K., Lloyd, S., Berens, C., Bowman, B., Myers, J., & Thompson, M. L. (2020). Urban upgrading and levels of interpersonal violence in Cape Town, *South Africa*: The violence prevention through urban upgrading programme. *Social Science & Medicine, 255*, 112978. https://doi.org/10.1016/j.socscimed.2020.112978

Mazeika, D. M., & Kumar, S. (2017). Do crime hot spots exist in developing countries? Evidence from India. *Journal of Quantitative Criminology, 33*(1), 45–61. https://doi.org/10.1007/s10940-016-9280-2

Openshaw, S. (1984). *The modifiable areal unit problem.* Norwich, England: GeoBooks.

O'Regan, C., Pikoli, V., Bawa, N., Sidaki, T., & Dissel, A. (2014). *Towards a safer Khayelitsha: The report of the commission of inquiry into allegations of police inefficiency and a breakdown in relations between SAPS and the community in Khayelitsha*, http://www.khayelitshacommission.org.za/, accessed 2 June 2022

Pierce, G., Spaar, S., & Briggs, L. R. (1988). *The character of police work strategic and tactical implications.* Center for Applied Social Research.

Pridemore, W. A., & Grubesic, T. H. (2013). Alcohol outlets and community levels of interpersonal violence: Spatial density, outlet type, and seriousness of assault. *Journal of Research in Crime and Delinquency, 50*(1), 132–159. https://doi.org/10.1177/0022427810397952

Reppetto, T. (1976). Crime prevention and the displacement phenomenon. *Crime and delinquency, 22*(2), 166–177. https://doi.org/10.1177/001112877602200020

Sampson, R. J., & Groves, W. (1989). Community structure and crime: Testing social disorganization theory. *American Journal of Sociology, 94*(4), 774–802. https://doi.org/10.1086/229068

Sampson, R. J., Raudenbush, S., & Earls, F. (1997). Neighborhoods and violent crime: A multilevel study of collective efficacy. *Science, 277*(5328), 918–924. https://doi.org/10.1126/science.277.5328.918

Sherman, L. W. (2022). "Test-as-you-go" for hot spots Policing: Continuous impact assessment with repeat crossover designs. *Cambridge Journal of Evidence-Based Policing, 6*, 25–41. https://doi.org/10.1007/s41887-022-00073-y

Sherman, L. W., Gartin, P. R., & Buerger, M. E. (1989). Hot spots of predatory crime: Routine activities and the criminology of place. *Criminology, 27*(1), 27–56. https://doi.org/10.1111/j.1745-9125.1989.tb00862.x

Statistics South Africa. (2011). http://www.statssa.gov.za/?s=Khayelitsha, accessed 2 June 2022

Steenbeek, W., & Weisburd, D. (2015). Where the action is in crime? An examination of variability of crime across different spatial units in The Hague, 2001–2009. *Journal of Quantitative Criminology, 32*(3), 449–469. https://doi.org/10.1007/s10940-015-9276-3

Stoltz, E. (2021). *Khayelitsha inquiry's recommendations into policing in the crime-infested township still ignored seven years on.* M&G Media Ltd. https://mg.co.za/news/2021-08-27-khayelitsha-inquirys-recommendations-into-policing-in-the-crime-infested-township-still-ignored-seven-years-on/, accessed 14 July 2022

Sullivan, J. P. (2020). *Gangs, criminal empires and military intervention in Cape Town's crime wars.* National Defence University Press.

Taylor, B., Koper, C., & Woods, D. (2011). A randomized controlled trial of different policing strategies at hot spots of violent crime. *Journal of Experimental Criminology, 7*(2), 149–181. https://doi.org/10.1007/s11292-010-9120-6

Uchida, C. D., & Swatt, M. L. (2013). Operation LASER and the effectiveness of hotspot patrol: A panel analysis. *Police Quarterly, 16*(3), 287–304. https://doi.org/10.1177/1098611113497044

Umar, F., Johnson, S. D., & Cheshire, J. A. (2021). Assessing the spatial concentration of urban crime: An insight from Nigeria. *Journal of Quantitative Criminology, 37*(3), 605–624. https://doi.org/10.1007/s10940-019-09448-3

Weisburd, D. (2015). The law of crime concentration and the criminology of place. *Criminology, 53*(2), 133–157. https://doi.org/10.1111/1745-9125.12070

Weisburd, D., & Amram, S. (2014). The law of concentrations of crime at place: The case of Tel Aviv-Jaffa. *Police Practice & Research, 15*(2), 101–114. https://doi.org/10.1080/15614263.2013.874169

Weisburd, D., Bushway, S., Lum, C., & Yang, S. M. (2004). Trajectories of crime at places: A Longitudinal study of street segments in the city of Seattle. *Criminology, 42*(2), 283–322. https://doi.org/10.1111/j.1745-9125.2004.tb00521.x

Weisburd, D., & Green, L. (1995). Policing drug hot spots: The Jersey City drug market analysis experiment. *Justice Quarterly*, *12*(4), 711–735. https://doi.org/10.1080/07418829500096261

Weisburd, D., Groff, E. R., & Yang, S. M. (2012). *The criminology of place: Street segments and our understanding of the crime problem*. Oxford University Press.

Weisburd, D., Morris, N. A., & Groff, E. R. (2009). Hot spots of juvenile crime: A longitudinal study of street segments in Seattle, Washington. *Journal of Quantitative Criminology*, *25*(4), 443–467. https://doi.org/10.1007/s10940-009-9075-9

Weisburd, D., & Telep, C. W. (2014). Hot spots policing: What we know and what we need to know. *Journal of Contemporary Criminal Justice*, *30*(2), 200–220. https://doi.org/10.1177/1043986214525083

Weisburd, D., & White, C. (2019). Hot spots of crime are not just hot spots of crime: Examining health outcomes at street segments. *Journal of Contemporary Criminal Justice*, *35*(2), 142–160. https://doi.org/10.1177/1043986219832132

Weisburd, D., Wyckoff, L., Ready, J., Eck, J., Hinkle, J., & Gajewski, F. (2006). Does crime just move around the corner? A controlled study of spatial displacement and diffusion of crime control benefits. *Criminology*, *44*(3), 549–592. https://doi.org/10.1111/j.1745-9125.2006.00057.x

Williams, S. A. (2015). *Do visits or time spent in hot spots patrol matter most? A randomized control trial in the west midlands police.* [Unpublished masters dissertation]. University of Cambridge.

World Economic Forum. (2016). *These are the world's five biggest slums*. https://www.weforum.org/agenda/2016/10/these-are-the-worlds-five-biggest-slums/, accessed 2 June 2022

Wuschke, K., Andresen, M. A., & Brantingham, P. L. (2021). Pathways of crime: Measuring crime concentration along urban roadways. *Canadian Geographer*, *65*(3), 267–280. https://doi.org/10.1111/cag.12676

A qualitative exploration of stress in a criminal investigations section

Kathleen E. Padilla, Alexis R. Rockwell and Jessica Huff

ABSTRACT

Traditional literature on stress in policing focuses on patrol officers and generalizes findings to other sections and ranks within the department. This fails to take into consideration that different sections may experience and manage stress in various ways. Following Dabney and colleagues (2013) examination of homicide investigators, the current study employs deductive coding to examine interviews from 21 investigators from financial, property, domestic violence, persons, and child crimes in the Criminal Investigations Section of a mid-sized Southwestern, United States police department. Findings were able to both replicate and expand upon Dabney and colleagues (2013) results, suggesting that even in a department that varies demographically and operationally from the original department, these investigators were exposed to and afflicted by many of the same stressors. While some of these stressors were similar to their patrol officer counterparts, investigators were further impacted by sources of stress that are unique to their specific role in the police organization (e.g., heavy caseloads, prolonged exposure to trauma, additional involvement with other criminal justice actors). Research and practical implications for departments – both international and domestic – in managing investigator stress are discussed.

Introduction

There is little question that the occupation of policing is a stressful one. While some organizational sources of stress in policing are like other bureaucratic organizations, there are operational stressors unique to law enforcement agencies. Organizational stressors, which transcend operational boundaries, can include bureaucratic red tape, excessive paperwork, or the lack of a supportive supervisor. Operational sources of stress could encompass writing traffic tickets, engaging in high-speed chases, or using force against citizens. Prior research has attempted to understand both sources of stress more thoroughly within police departments, and generally finds that organizational stressors are rated as more impactful than operational stressors by a ratio of 6:1 (Brown & Campbell, 1990). With the shifting law enforcement climate, including increased scrutiny from communities, social media, and governmental pressures resulting from excessive force incidents, there is reason to believe that operational stressors may now be increasing their impact on police officers (Denk-Florea et al., 2020). It is with these concerns in mind that both operational and organizational sources of stress should be accounted for when examining police officers' day-to-day duties and perceptions (Rabbing et al., 2022).

Research on police officer stress typically focuses on patrol or line officers. Given line officers account for most personnel within a police department and engage with the public the most, little reason has been given for studies to look beyond this level. Indeed, only between 11% and 15% of police personnel nationwide work in a detective or investigations role (Goodison, 2022). This results in sources of stress for police officers being generalized from patrol officers across all other levels of the department, thereby removing potential variation among ranks and units within these agencies. Much less is known about stress in other ranks or units within police departments. As officers move from patrol to specialized assignments or management-level ranks, their sources of stress may shift to show other organizational and operational stressors as more prevalent (Dabney et al., 2013; Padilla, 2016).

The current study addresses these issues by replicating a qualitative examination of stress in a homicide unit (Dabney et al., 2013) and examines sources of stress among investigators within the Criminal Investigations Section (CIS) of a mid-size Southwestern, United States police department. This specialized unit deals with a variety of assignments, including crimes against persons, sex crimes against both adults and children, finance, and property crimes. Explicitly, we sought to examine the sources of operational and organizational stressors felt by 21 investigators working in these assignments in the CIS using a modified version of Dabney and colleague's homicide detective interview guide.

Stress in policing

Sources of stress related to law enforcement have been well established (Anshel, 2000; Collins & Gibbs, 2003; Spielberger et al., 1981; Violanti & Aron, 1995), though the levels of stress associated with police work has generally been mixed (Carelton et al., 2018; Collins & Gibbs, 2003; Salinas & Webb, 2018). What is consistent in most policing literature is that officers tend to classify their stress into two categories: (1) stressors caused by the organization itself; and (2) those inherent to the operations of policing (Brown & Campbell, 1990; Collins & Gibbs, 2003; Violanti & Aron, 1993) Most self-report survey studies on police stress find that stress due to the organization itself - the bureaucratic structure or the high levels of supervision - tend to be more impactful in the lives of officers (Brown & Campbell, 1990; Collins & Gibbs, 2003; Violanti & Aron, 1993). In some cases, these organizational features are four to six times more stressful than operational features (Brown & Campbell, 1990; Violanti & Aron, 1993). It could be argued that because risks inherent to the job itself were expected from officers, those risks then resulted in less unanticipated stress.

Overall, consequences of stress can be seen in various dimensions of police life, with the individual officer themselves, their families, and the departments potentially being impacted. Some of the psychological consequences of prolonged stress on police officers include depression, post-traumatic stress disorder, anxiety, and exhaustion (Burns et al., 2008; Gershon et al., 2009; MacEachern et al., 2019; Stinchcomb, 2004). These can all manifest into physiological symptoms when attempts to manage these emotional consequences are not handled properly (Brady, 2012). Further physiological consequences include increased rates of cardiovascular disease and high blood pressure (Franke et al., 2002; President's Task Force, 2015), as well as elevated levels of insomnia and chronic pain problems (Gershon et al., 2009). In Canada, roughly 45% of first responders (i.e., dispatchers, firefighters, paramedics, and police officers) were reported to have positive screens for 'clinically significant symptom clusters consistent with 1 or more mental disorders' (Carleton et al., 2018). Additional extreme consequences of mismanaged stress can include suicidal ideation and suicide (Violanti et al., 2018), with officer deaths by suicide surpassing accidental or felonious deaths (Blue H.E.L.P., 2020; Officer Down Memorial Page, 2020; O'hara, 2017). Family life is also at risk of being disrupted due to ill-managed stress, with higher rates of divorce (Miller, 2007; Nordlicht, 1979) and domestic violence among officers (Gibson et al., 2001;

Miller, 2007; Violanti & Aron, 1995) when compared to the general population. Regarding consequences for the police department itself, officers who accumulate high levels of stress – in correlation with limited supervisor support, cohesiveness within the department, and opportunities for promotion – are less committed to the department and thus have higher turnover rates (Jaramillo et al., 2005). Aside from the turnover risks of stressed officers, their health consequences can hurt the department as well, manifesting in numerous sick days, limiting resources, and lowering performance of the department (Gershon et al., 2009; President's Task Force, 2015).

Stress and specialized units

The limited research on stress among officers within specialized units finds that members of specialized units accumulate stress at different levels and from alternative sources than their patrol officer counterparts (Dabney et al., 2013; Denk-Florea et al., 2020; Krause, 2009; Sewell, 1994; Van Patten & Burke, 2001). Most of this stress originates as a result of the particular focus surrounding investigation of these specialized crimes, such as child abuse cases and homicides (Brady, 2012; Burns et al., 2008; MacEachern et al., 2019; Roth & Vivona, 2010). Similar to those in patrol, stress among officers within a specialized unit can also be categorized into both organizational and operational stressors.

Organizationally, there is often a disproportionate ratio between homicide investigators and the rest of the department (Sewell, 1994). These units are often seen as the 'natural habitat of [the] rarified species, the thinking cop' (Simon, 1991, p. 17), and thus are held with high regard. Investigators are often forced to work odd hours (Krause, 2009) and are pressured to resolve cases quickly while still being available to respond to new calls (Sewell, 1994). Further, the department often has a higher priority than one's personal life, which can cause considerable conflict at home for many of these investigators (Miller, 2007). Members of these units often do not perceive other criminal justice system components as legitimate, including prosecutors who may be reluctant to move forward with cases, due to lack of evidence (Burns et al., 2008), or social support services who failed to intervene in situations before they escalate to requiring homicide investigator involvement (Burns et al., 2008; Sewell, 1994). Additionally, some of the factors influencing risk amongst investigators include the frequency, duration, and type or intensity of exposure, the perceived control over the source of stress, and the coping strategies one has (Burns et al., 2008; Krause, 2009; MacEachern et al., 2019).

These organizational factors exacerbate stress felt by investigators from other sources (Henry, 1995; Krause, 2009; Sewell, 1994). There tends to be an inherent fear of disappointing victims' families and investigators are often left to deal with loved ones of the victim without having extensive training in delivering death notifications or grief processing (Sewell, 1994). Many of these investigators 'feel called to the work, voice a firm unwillingness to "abandon" the victims by changing assignments, and grow numb to the strains inherent in this unique activity' (Krause, 2009, p. 24). Cases of exposure to distressing imagery, like those inherent to crimes against children, can lead to both psychological and physiological responses (Cubitt & Judges, 2018; Denk-Florea et al., 2020). Some of these responses in prior qualitative studies closely resembled PTSD symptomology for short periods of time, including flashbacks and feelings shock and disgust (Denk-Florea et al., 2020). In addition to the victim's family, investigators must often manage the media coverage of the crime scene and ensure accurate and appropriate information is being released (Dabney et al., 2013).

Short-term coping strategies for homicide and high-risk investigators can be paralleled to how other first responders cope with death and include socialized desensitization in the academy through graphic photos or videos or sharing their experiences with coworkers or individuals who have similar experiences (Carleton et al., 2018; Denk-Florea et al., 2020; Salinas & Webb, 2018). Specifically, Carleton and colleagues (2018) highlight that Canadian first responders experience 'regular exposure to ... threatened or actual physical assaults' (p. 55) and other job-specific operational stressors which are correlated with increases in mental health disorders. When compared internationally, anywhere from 10% to 35% of first responders experience mental health disorders resulting from both operational and organizational stressors (Carleton et al., 2018). Additionally, investigators are known to reward lack of affect in the field and look down on those who display emotions. Dark humor and the use of operational jargon are common among members of these units as well (Roth & Vivona, 2010; Sewell, 1994; Van Patten & Burke, 2001).

Departmentally, long-term coping strategies can include proactive approaches, such as creating a positive organizational environment that encourages communication, trust, and the understanding of the impact that individual self-care can have on organizational self-care, and regular job rotation (Birch et al., 2021; Salinas & Webb, 2018; Sewell, 1994). Retroactively, mandatory critical incident debriefings, providing psychologists and grief counselors that are familiar with the work of homicide investigators, and including programs geared towards officer-specific resilience interventions could be beneficial to ensure that investigators understand the realities of their work as well as increase their psychological tool-belt to cope with those realities (Eddy et al., 2021; Salinas & Webb, 2018; Sewell, 1994).

Present study

The current paper seeks to add to the literature by providing a qualitative replication, exploring sources of stress among officers and detectives within a Criminal Investigations Section (CIS) of a mid-size Southwestern, United States police department. Using a modified version of Dabney et al. (2013) homicide detective interview guide, interviews with 21 members of a CIS were conducted. The members of this department vary in rank, assignment, tenure, gender, and race. The researchers sought to understand sources of stress more thoroughly from investigators in a specialized unit, one that deals with crimes against persons, including sex crimes against adults and children, assaults, and homicide, in addition to financial and property crimes. Prior work by Sewell (1994) provided a framework for stress experienced by homicide investigators, which was empirically examined by Dabney and colleagues (2013). Here, we seek to examine if this framework remains valid when we examine a broader range of investigators, beyond just looking at those working homicides. Importantly, prior empirical research has highlighted that, quantitatively, officers and investigators within this section have significantly higher levels of organizational and operational stress compared to officers within the department generally, particularly as it related to feelings of paranoia about their safety or their families' safety, making critical on-the-spot decisions, excessive paperwork, inadequate salary, and insufficient manpower to adequately handle a job (Padilla, 2016). It is thereby important to better understand the unique experiences of these members to more effectively provide assistance.

Methods

Sample

The current study took place in a mid-sized Southwestern police department which employed approximately 180 sworn officers in 2016 and covers 77 square miles.[1] In 2016, the sample city had a violent crime rate of 251 per 100,000, well below the national average of 386.3 per 100,000 (UCR, 2016). The department was approximately 92% male (well below the national average for female representation), and 51% Hispanic. The Criminal Investigations Section (CIS) this study is situated within was also majority male and majority Hispanic. Their tenure in CIS ranged from approximately 6 months to 14 years, with an average tenure length of 4.48 years. The investigators in this sample had a total tenure in law enforcement range of 4 years to 20 years, with an average of 14.52 years. A majority of the sample was married and/or had children, and a majority had at least some college education, with about a quarter having at least a Bachelor's degree. Table 1 highlights the

Table 1. Sample Demographics.

	Frequency or Mean
Gender (Male)	90.48%
Age	40.76 years
Race/Ethnicity	
White	38.10%
Hispanic	57.14%
Black/African American	4.76%
Marital Status (Married)	85.71%
Child Status (Have Children)	85.71%
Education	
High School/GED	9.52%
Some College	42.86%
Associate's Degree	14.29%
Bachelor's Degree	23.81%
Master's Degree	9.52%
Tenure in CIS	4.48 years
Tenure in Law Enforcement	14.52 years
Tenure Prior to CIS Assignment	10.04 years
Role	
Investigator	85.71%
Supervisor	14.29%
Interview Time	34.29 minutes

Respondents will be denoted with an assigned number (e.g., 'R1,' 'R2').

demographics of the 21 respondents in the sample. Specific units represented within CIS include finance crimes, property crimes, crimes against persons, and crimes against children. It is important to note that while these investigators worked in particular units within CIS, when they were on-call, they could all be assigned any kind of case. That is, a crimes against persons detective could be handed a finance case, and vice versa. Within CIS, there are approximately 5 investigators assigned to each section (crimes against persons, crimes against children, finance crimes, and property crimes), with 2 sergeants and 1 lieutenant.

Procedure

The original interview guide utilized by Dabney and colleagues in their 2013 study was acquired and modified for the current study. Dabney et al. (2013) conducted one-on-one interviews with homicide investigators during ride-alongs. The current study modified that for a workplace setting, occurring in either the investigators' offices or in the CIS conference room, creating more structure to the questioning procedure. This study received approval from the institutional review board of the lead researcher's university, in addition to receiving approval from both the police department chief and the Section lieutenant. All potential respondents were recruited for participation in their offices, and all approached investigators agreed to participate, either at that time, or at a future scheduled time. Where applicable, the respondent's officemate left the room so that all interviews were one-on-one, between the respondent and the lead author. Office doors were closed at the discretion of the investigator to ensure privacy during the interview. This procedure allowed the investigators some flexibility with their duties at scenes, interviewing witnesses or victims, or appearing in court. Semi-structured interviews were conducted with the 21 investigators during a week-long period in December 2016.

Investigators were asked a broad range of questions, including their motivation for entering law enforcement and joining CIS, the perceived costs and rewards of being an investigator, reactions upon arriving to crime scenes, organizational and operational factors that may impact their job, sources and consequences of stress, coping with stress, and what the department could be doing to better support investigators and officers who want to become investigators. All questions were open-ended to encourage a deeper discussion of each aspect. All interviews were audio-recorded, and consent was captured on audio. Interviews lasted between 18 and 67 min, averaging approximately 35 min. The length of respondent interviews ranged due to the veracity and willingness of each respondent to discuss the content. Certainly, some respondents were more open and conversational than others.[2] The full interview guide is available upon request.

Analytic plan

All interviews were transcribed by a graduate student and checked for accuracy by the lead author. Due to the goal of the current study being to replicate and expand upon Dabney et al. (2013) study, the current study employs a deductive coding approach where topic areas and codes had been determined apriori. That is, the areas of interest in the current study are organizational and operational (framed as occupational in Dabney et al., 2013) sources of stress, as identified by the inductive thematic coding in Dabney et al.'s (2013) work. Replication and novel themes were identified using Microsoft Word (La Pelle, 2004).

Results[3]

As indicated, the present study was interested in sources of stress among investigators in a Criminal Investigations Section (CIS), in an effort to replicate prior research. Dabney and colleagues (2013) highlighted seven categories of stress, stemming from both operational and organizational sources. These included: working crime scenes, time pressures, paperwork demands, adjudication demands, administrative pressure, unit culture, and external demands. The findings of the current study were consistent for all seven of these categories. The subsequent sections are organized to provide evidence for these replicated findings and additional context to better understand each area of interest.

Operational sources of stress

In line with Dabney's et al. (2013) work, operational stress could be identified as stemming from arriving to and working crime scenes, managing time pressures, paperwork and report demands, and adjudication and court demands. The following discussion is organized into three subsections, consistent with Dabney and colleagues (2013) presentation: working crime scenes, time pressures and paperwork demands, and adjudication demands.

Working crime scenes

Investigators' involvement in active crime scenes is magnified when they are on call and responsible for responding to any case that comes in. When asked about the process they go through upon arriving at crime scenes, one investigator noted:

> We'll get some sort of a little bit of a heads up, like what kind of call we're responding to, so you kinda already start getting, you know, mental prep. Like, there's a difference between, say a felony shoplifter amount for TVs at Target, as opposed to somebody who just, you know just ran somebody over on purpose and killed 'em or almost killed 'em, you know? So, it's just a different thought process. (R5).

These procedures appear to serve a protective function for the investigators, both in terms of helping regulate their emotions and keeping their mentality sharp and alert to be most effective in managing that scene. The potential for emotions, particularly for crime scenes involving children, to 'cloud [their] train of thought' (R18) or 'clog [their] decision-making' (R10) was a salient concern among these investigators. This often led to second guessing one's own decisions after the fact, which, as one financial crimes investigator noted, isn't 'necessarily a bad thing . . . it keeps you on your toes' (R9).

This desire to attain emotional neutrality when arriving to scenes resulted in certain levels of dissociation and disconnect between the investigators and the victims and families of victims on scene. One domestic violence investigator noted,

> A lot of 'em don't bother me. You know in a logical sense, I can tell that 'hey, maybe this is pretty bad,' you know my brain knows that. As a person I know that, that this is a bad situation or this is a sad situation or this is an urgent situation, but I mean past that, it just, it kinda, it takes a specific call to really get to me. (R12).

This sentiment was further exemplified by a crimes against children investigator, who articulated that 'if you start taking it personal it's gonna eat you up . . . you gotta just realize regardless of how terrible someone was to someone else, you can't look at it like it was against you' (R2).

From the supervisor's point of view, arriving to and managing crime scenes takes a different approach, one that was concerned predominately with the logistical aspects of the scene and case. This supervisor, who was relatively new to CIS, highlighted the following:

> As a [supervisor] I think you have to remove yourself one step from the cases, from the detectives, from the public, and you almost have to see more of a bigger picture. So, you're taking, like a step back. Whereas, opposed to a detective, you're in it, this is your case and you're in it, you're working it. The thing is, as a supervisor, you take that step back and you're seeing, you know how is this effecting our department, how is this effecting our city, you know, how is this effecting our detectives, you know, what can we do to resolve these problems? (R16).

Time pressures and paperwork demands

Among the investigators in this department, the time pressures associated with high caseloads and paperwork demands was palpable. While discussed more thoroughly below, the assignment process for cases includes several levels of screening for suitability and appropriate unit placement. In this Section, investigators who are new begin in the crimes against children unit, as that is typically the most backlogged unit. From there, most investigators only spend approximately two years in that unit before they are rotated out and into a new unit. As mentioned by one investigator who had moved into financial crimes, crimes against children cases 'wear on your conscience' (R9), and these sentiments were especially noted by those who had children of their own. In particular, feelings of not having adequate time to spend on each case, due to the large number of cases, were prevalent. The pressures to manage high caseloads in this unit was noted by two investigators, both of whom had begun their CIS career in crimes against children, and had since rotated out:

> Because there's so many, you know, there's a sense that you've gotta rush through these things to get onto the next because they don't go away, they only add up. So, you can get 3 in one day, 3 referrals in a day, and close out 1 case, well now you're plus 2, and the next day you get 3, close out 1 and now you're plus 4, so that can get a bit overwhelming. (R10).

> When I was in crimes against children I was just overwhelmed. You could not give the correct attention to these cases and that one was even more severe because you're having, not only lives, but children's lives that you're dealing with, which to me it would make it ten-fold. (R21).

Particularly as it relates to the paperwork demands that no doubt add to the struggle to spend adequate time on cases, these investigators understood the reality that so much of what they do and how they 'catch the bad guy,' entails being able to get the vast amount of required paperwork done in an organized, readable, and timely manner. To that end, when navigating the pressures of paperwork demands, one property crimes investigator highlighted that paperwork truly was a key aspect of case management:

> If you don't work on your cases and you don't solve them, no one really cares, they just keep calling up. To the point where you're drowning, and when you feel like you're getting caught up, you get an influx of reports so to get 'em solved and get 'em going, that's, that's one of the major ones. (R18).

In terms of how to get through the influx of reports, a financial crimes investigator noted that they take a minute to calm themselves, and 'tell myself, you know what, I can't do it all right away, so I prioritize it' (R3). It is important to note, that investigators in property and finance crimes units typically have caseloads that are two to three times that of those in persons-based units.

Beyond working in the crimes against children unit, the time pressures associated with managing high caseloads was something that these investigators often had to relay to other stakeholders in the cases and was something that could be felt from both the investigators and the supervisors. From the supervisor side, the screening process helps investigators manage their time, but the supervisors are aware that they "can't give 'em [all] out because they'll never get anything done. They'll be inundated with too many reports" (R16). From the investigator side, the personal pressure that is added because of these time constraints results in investigators worrying about not doing enough. As one investigator highlighted:

> I don't want to screw over my victim or like fuck over my victim because I didn't do something on time. So, that's my, that's my biggest feeling with the caseload if it gets too much, am I gonna be able to do everything? (R12).

An additional area related to time pressures and constraints was the impact of scheduling and overtime. The emphasis on scheduling and overtime in the current study could likely be an artifact of the recent policy changes that took the Section from 4/10s (10-hour shifts, 4 days a week) to 5/8s (8-hour shifts, 5 days a week) and altered their overtime schedule. Previously, investigators were on 7-day callouts every 6 weeks. That is, every 6 weeks, an investigator was on-call from one Friday to the following Friday. This grueling schedule left investigators running on fumes and was powerfully highlighted by several investigators:

> There was times that you could get your ass totally handed to you come Friday and you wouldn't even be home 'til Sunday, and you're literally, you're just, you're almost to the point where you're hallucinating, you're in bad shape. (R19).

> You could be out all night and have to still come to work during the day, and you get called out, so there's times where you haven't slept in 24 hours, and you know and there's times when you feel like you're under the influence because you're probably at .02 after 24 hours of no sleep. (R6).

While the potential for no sleep still exists in the current set-up, the argument was that because it was now only 24 h every 10 days, you could manage the lack of sleep much more reasonably. Additionally, as with all policies, there are downsides to even the most positive changes. One investigator noted, 'I love the fact that it's just one day as opposed to the weeks that we used to work, or the week, but the good thing about working that week was that you would have at least six weeks off' (R11). That is, the investigators alluded to being able to plan more activities and events with their families when they *knew* that they would have six weeks of their normal work schedule, as opposed to having to make alternative arrangements every ten days.

Adjudication demands

Moving beyond the confines of the police department, investigators spend a substantial amount of time working with, and oftentimes at the whim of, prosecutors and other legal actors. Investigators in this study highlighted different points of the adjudication process where they felt heightened levels of stress. Starting before a district attorney (DA) even receives a case, one crimes against children investigator noted that 'I like to be more thorough when it comes to charging someone or know ... for my own ... I guess peace of mind that the person I am charging definitely did this' (R2).

Once a case is in the hands of the legal team, investigators may be asked to provide *additional* disclosures or case materials, and when this is done at the drop of the hat, so to speak, this resulted in added stress. One crimes against persons investigator discussed that this could be particularly stressful if they needed to retrieve the case materials from the lab or another Section that has different processes and procedures (R6). One aspect that was directly identified by Dabney and colleagues (2013) was the potential to 'get hammered in court' (p. 824). Indeed, one veteran crimes against persons investigator poignantly noted the pressures to put together the best possible case for fear of repercussions at trial:

> When you're in a trial and they're grilling you on the stand on shortcomings of a case, that gets published in the paper, and that sucks, 'cause your name is tagged to it. (R10).

Beyond this concern, many of the investigators highlighted the very real potential for outcomes that they felt were not in line with the case or the effort they put into the case. That is, when an individual case does not move forward, results in a dismissal, or results in a sentence that they feel is disproportionate to the damage they witnessed resulting from the offense. As demonstrated by a property crimes investigator:

> Hey, I put in hours upon hours upon hours of work and I have 3 huge boxes of bank documents that I sifted through. A lot of it I did on regular time and overtime because I picked up that case when a guy went on maternity, paternity leave and so I had to work it as overtime which was great for me because it gave me extra money, but what did it cost me in overtime and the department in time to the sentence that [they] actually received? Guy lost a business, ten people lost their jobs, and we got two years out of it? (R14).

Organizational sources of stress

While the operational sources of stress were well-documented among this sample, they were types of stress that were more or less expected or anticipated when the respondents joined CIS. They appeared to be less prepared for the organizational factors that impacted their job satisfaction and efficacy. In line with (Dabney et al., 2013) study, the investigators noted both internal and external pressures and demands related to closing their cases. What was differentially highlighted, as compared to Dabney and colleagues' (2013) work, was the unit culture, which will be discussed further below. The following discussion is organized into three subsections, consistent with Dabney and colleagues (2013) presentation: administrative pressures, external pressures and demands, and unit culture.

Administrative pressures

Within the CIS, the procedure for case assignment entails a case being screened by civilian staff to ensure it is a matter for an investigator, as opposed to another member of the department; those cases make it to the desk of a sergeant, who then screens it for suitability and prioritizes it before assigning it to an investigator in the appropriate section. This leaves investigators with a range of open cases, from 10 to 20 for those in persons-based sections, to 30–40 for those in finance/property sections. This is all done in conjunction with investigators being on call for that 24-hour period, every 10 days, with those cases typically taking priority over the current roster of cases.

In those cases that have particularly high priority, it becomes important to the supervisors and administrators for the case to be handled swiftly and appropriately. One investigator, who was rather seasoned in terms of law enforcement tenure overall, but was fairly new to CIS, noted, 'I think the worst stress and pressure in law enforcement doesn't come from ... criminals, doesn't come from victims, or investigations, it comes from the administration and the supervisors and people trying to please their higher ups' (R2). This was perceived by other investigators, and while some politically driven cases garnered heightened attention, the investigators typically only felt pressure from their immediate supervisors when it was clear that their caseload was backlogged.

For those who worked in a supervisory role, they generally described a hands-off approach to case management taken in CIS. One supervisor specifically highlighted his 'take care of my people and... ask for forgiveness later' (R4) mentality, acknowledging their position more as a logistical supporter versus a micro-manager. This is something that was noted and seemingly appreciated by the investigators that worked under them. Indeed, one financial crimes investigator noted, 'I do my job and people leave me alone' (R19). By and large, however, the pressures placed on individuals in this Section were not the most prominent source of stress discussed by the respondents, potentially explained by the increased autonomy and general lack of micro-managing that is experienced by individuals who work within investigations.

External pressures and demands

In line with Dabney and colleagues' (2013) discussion, the investigators in this study discussed, at length, their experiences with the media and judicial system, as well as the victims and families of victims. When it came to media pressures and the way the media represents law enforcement in general, most of the investigators held less than favorable attitudes. Stemming largely from a perceived incomplete picture being presented to the public, one investigator was sure to note how this differentiated from their time in patrol, that because '[they're] not the one being videotaped on the side of the road, [they] don't feel it anymore' (R12).

Other investigators noted the potential impact of the media and their role in information dissemination, in that 'they're gonna do their job and they're gonna pull what they can from us' (R18). This was exemplified with one supervisor highlighting the conflict they faced related to information dissemination:

> It's always a constant battle of, I wanna put out everything that we possibly could but they don't like it 'cause it could damage the case, could expose the victim, so there are those struggles almost on a daily basis. You know, what do we release? What do we tell people? What can we tell people? What should we be telling people? (R1).

While this type of experience could be considered a tactical one related to case preservation, other investigators noted more emotionally charged experiences, with pleas of victims or families of victims for more information, more progress, and more results. Whether it was a call attempting to persuade an investigator to not move forward with a case, or an unannounced visitor pushing them to prosecute (not understanding that it is not their call to prosecute), one financial crimes investigator noted that they must focus to 'not get emotionally involved with them to the point where [they're] letting them guide through [the] investigation' (R9). This investigator further highlighted that because they saw these cases on a regular basis, effectively desensitizing them to their impact, they were still aware that for those victims or families of victims, it may have been the worst day of their life.

Unit culture

While Dabney and colleagues (2013) discussed a culture that focused on continuous engagement between members of the homicide unit, this did not appear to be the case in the current study. Certainly, it is important to note that unit culture and police culture more broadly are not homogenous and there is substantial variation between states, cities, departments, sections, etc. that would impact the culture within any specific unit (see Crank, 2014; Paoline & Terrill, 2013). What was described in the current study was more individualistic in nature, and while there was certainly a competitive nature alluded to from the respondents, it was more a pressure imposed on oneself to do better, rather than jabs between coworkers to do better.

One explanation could be the diversity of investigators within CIS, as compared to the homicide unit Dabney and colleagues focused on. This Section houses four types of investigators: finance, property, crimes against persons, and crimes against children, that handle substantively different types of cases and that can require vastly different work hours or strategies. In this Section, then, there appeared to be little value in comparing caseloads. Indeed, a property crimes investigator noted that 'there's some cases that take priority over others, crimes against persons will take priority over property' (R15). While this was in reference to managing community expectations, it was similarly alluded to when an investigator is on-call. What is more, while one investigator noted the perception of 'cliques' within CIS, they also noted it was likely to be a result of the Section being predominately male, with only two female investigators, both assigned to stereotypically female caseloads: crimes against persons (with a focus on domestic violence) and crimes against children.

A particular aspect of unit culture that was referenced, was how different 'being back here' was to being on patrol, and the general lack of understanding from officers in other Sections. This sentiment was highlighted by several investigators, with feelings that 'they [patrol] don't understand what we do back here' (R6) and 'they [patrol] also don't want to learn about it' (R13). Especially when it came to dealing with crime scenes, the investigators in this study alluded to being in an entirely different world. The following two excerpts from a financial crimes investigator and a crimes against persons investigator saliently highlight the disparities between patrol and CIS:

> When you're on patrol, you go to a call, you handle it you're done. So, you don't worry about it anymore. Back here, the to-do list is just never ending. (R11).

> We deal with a whole lot more than first responders do, just because we get a lot of it. First responders will be, they'll see the actual, let's say like a death. That might be the only death that they'll see for months. We see it on a continuous basis. Because we're the ones that go out and respond to, take care of, we have to be there for the family, so we see all the emotions with the family. (R6).

Importantly, the investigators were acutely aware of these differences between patrol and investigations, as well as the contrast in their own expectations versus reality of what CIS is. One property crimes investigator detailed the jarring disconnect between what they thought they were prepared for, versus what the job entailed:

> I thought that it was gonna be basically . . . what I needed to do on patrol. And when I came back here it was nothing like that. It was a lot harder; it was a lot more detail that I needed to learn, it was a lot of steps that we had no idea had to be done on patrol, things that we had to do with the district attorney's office, other agencies. How to testify. You testify on patrol but it's different, the way you interview people is different. The techniques that you use, all the techniques are different. Assignments that you do to do an investigation. Things like setting up bait cars, wire taps, all these different things that I had no experience with on patrol and it was a lot different, a lot different job. (R15).

Discussion

This study is one of the first qualitative replications in policing literature. Using the same interview instrument as Dabney's et al. (2013) in an assessment of stressors among investigators in a Homicide Unit, the current results identified the same predominant themes among investigators in a Criminal Investigations Section – despite the different types of investigation units involved in each study, the different police organizations under study, and different time periods. Although qualitative research is intended to be context specific and is not subject to the same concerns about replicability as quantitative work by nature, our findings speak to the persistence and commonality of factors that contribute to stress among police investigators across time, geography, and organizational cultures. This is particularly notable given dramatic changes in the policing climate between the interviews conducted by Dabney's et al. (2013) in 2009 and the current interviews which were conducted in 2016.

Further, these results highlight important variation in operational and organizational stressors between patrol officers and investigators. Given that most research evaluating stress among police officers focuses on line-level officers, this is an important contribution to understanding how different job functions within a police organization have differential influences on mental health. Namely, patrol officers respond to initial scenes for a wide variety of incidents to provide immediate police responses, while investigators routinely respond to traumatic events and must continue to engage with the same case over a long period of time. The potential for consistent exposure to trauma among investigators, regardless of primary assignment, is likely to contribute to the suicide rates (Violanti et al., 2018), incidents of domestic violence (Miller, 2007), and turnover rates (Jaramillo et al., 2005) among law enforcement officers more broadly. Our results, therefore, contribute an important understanding of factors that increase investigator stress, which are inherently different from patrol officers, and highlight avenues for addressing those stressors. Although some of the same organizational and operational stressors are experienced by all police officers within an organization, like Dabney and colleagues (2013), our results suggest that some stressors experienced by investigators are distinct to their role and are unlikely to impact patrol officers who do not perform the same job functions. For example, while patrol officers experience stress related to uncertainty about what each individual call-for-service could lead to, every call that a crimes against persons investigator responds to involve violence. This leads to repeated exposure to traumatic events for these investigators, whereas a patrol officer might respond to these types of incidents very infrequently. Many of our respondents discussed the challenge of managing multiple cases over long periods of time, while devoting sufficient attention to building the strongest possible case for each. These stressors are unique to investigators, who must continue to engage with the same case for several months or years, while a patrol officer who responded to the same incident would simply move on to the next call.

The influence of operational stressors

Prior research confirms that policing is a stressful occupation. That is, certain job expectations that are unique to being a police officer more generally, and an investigator specifically, lead to operationally specific stress. However, the operational stressors experienced by investigators in this study were unique to their specific job expectations, as opposed to operational stressors experienced by police officers more generally (e.g., enforcing laws, making arrests, etc.). Though homicide investigators in Dabney's et al. (2013) study often discussed challenges managing crime scenes and preserving evidence, investigators in this study talked more about mentally preparing to deal with a traumatic event and managing their emotional responses. Investigators choose to pursue a career in the CIS. As such, they expect to deal with emotional cases on a routine basis and might be particularly well-suited to manage these unique operational stressors. Further, individual officers differ in their levels of resilience for exposure to traumatic incidents. These internal differences in resilience could influence whether an officer self-selects into the CIS as well as their ability to manage exposure to traumatic cases once they are in the CIS. It is important to note that the salience of stress related to responding to traumatic events is not as simple as the frequency of exposure to these incidents, but also to individual propensity for managing these emotionally charged incidents. While investigators might experience these events more routinely than patrol officers, that does not mean that patrol officers do not need emotional support when they encounter these incidents.

Other operational stressors that were highlighted involved time pressures, paperwork, and adjudication. Each of these stressors are uniquely experienced by investigators who are expected to take ownership over their assigned cases. As such, the onus to complete an investigation and close a case rests solidly on their shoulders. Further, to ensure that an investigation is successful, they also feel tremendous pressure to properly complete paperwork to support their decisions and conclusions. All of this is meant to culminate in a criminal conviction. Patrol officers who serve as initial responders to these incidents do not experience the same operational pressures related to long-term case outcomes. Given high caseloads within the different sections of the CIS, these investigators were under tremendous pressure to resolve cases to prevent acquiring an even larger caseload. These challenges are interrelated, resulting in investigators feeling immense pressure from the initiation of a case through its conclusion because of the nature of their work.

The influence of organizational stressors

Prior policing studies have found that organizational stressors, which can transcend operational boundaries, are more salient than operational stressors (Brown & Campbell, 1990; Violanti & Aron, 1993). Namely, organizational stressors refer to challenges associated with working in a bureaucratic organization, which are not unique to policing but are experienced by employees in a wide range of occupations (e.g., pressure from supervisors). Again, consistent with Dabney and colleagues (2013), organizational stressors in our study related to administrative pressures and external pressures to resolve cases. Investigators in the CIS are responsible for resolving cases that involve substantial physical and financial harm to victims. As such, investigators experience consistent pressure from supervisors within the CIS and executive leadership to resolve cases. Further, consistent with prior research, this pressure to resolve cases is compounded by external pressure from victims and families, the media and court personnel (Dabney et al., 2013; Sewell, 1994). This complex network of individuals has diverse interests in the resolution of the case – everything from resolving personal harm to ensuring that proper police procedures are followed to facilitate a successful conviction. As the primary individuals responsible for these cases, investigators are uniquely positioned within the police organization and experience a myriad of pressures in a much different way than patrol officers, police supervisors, or other personnel who do not have these responsibilities. While investigators who select into the CIS might be prepared for the operational stress associated with managing emotional cases, they might be less prepared for the organizational pressures to effectively manage their caseload.

While many of the themes identified in the current study coincide with prior research conducted by Dabney and colleagues (2013), there were major differences in stress related to organizational culture within these separate investigative units. Although homicide investigators in the Dabney's et al. (2013) study reported severe internal competition to solve cases, this competition was not identified among CIS investigators in the present study. CIS investigators reported feeling internal pressure to complete cases to keep their caseloads low and to serve victims but did not mention that they were competing with others in their unit, whether they were assigned to the same section within the CIS or not. This difference could also be attributed to the fact that the homicide unit had a centrally located bulletin board that specifically listed each investigator by name along with their number of open cases. This made it readily apparent which homicide investigators were closing cases and which were not. In the CIS unit examined in the current study, this practice was not in place. In fact, because the CIS is responsible for multiple types of cases and individual investigators are rotated through different assignments on a fairly regular basis (every few years), this alleviated both the emotional toll of working on some types of cases and increased understanding among investigators about the various challenges experienced in each section and how those challenges contribute to an investigator's caseload.

Limitations and future directions

Like all research, this study is not without limitations. Although the themes identified in the current study aligned with those in the original Dabney's et al. (2013) assessment, the overall generalizability of this study remains an open question. It was also not possible to compare how similar the agency examined in the current study is to the agency examined in the original Dabney's et al. (2013) study, which was described as a metropolitan police department with about 2,000 sworn officers. The CIS in the current study is housed in a smaller police department and investigates a broader range of offenses, as opposed to just homicide. Broader differences in these agencies and units could lead to the distinct organizational and operational stressors we identified, compared to the original study. However, that two departments that vary greatly in composition and assignment are experiencing many of the same stressors is interesting to note. Given the nature of qualitative work, which is meant to provide a depth of responses that often necessitates ensuring anonymity for study participants, it is challenging to compare the specific characteristics of the respondents in Dabney's et al. (2013) to those in the current study. This limitation is likely to face future qualitative replications as well.

Additionally, due to the anonymous nature of the original department and their selection criteria into specialty units such as the homicide unit, as well as the public unavailability of such criteria of the current study site, there is much we do not know related to how the criteria for entrance into such specialty units may impact the susceptibility to and resilience of certain workplace stressors. This presents an opportunity for future research to examine.

Though qualitative studies are not intended to be generalizable, but are instead meant to provide rich contextual information, replicating these studies in other places remains an important avenue for understanding sources of police stress. While the investigative section in this study, along with the broader department and city are both racially and ethnically diverse, these findings can only speak to patterns within one investigative section, in one department, in one city in the U.S. Additional studies examining stress among investigators in different cities, states, countries, and with different caseloads should be considered. These additional studies would further benefit from the use of both qualitative and quantitative methodologies to continue to identify factors that contribute to stress and to inform the development of survey instruments intended to assess the salience of those stressors. Additionally, though officers provided candid information about sensitive topics during their interviews, it is not possible to assess how transparent these officers truly were in their responses.

Policy implications and conclusions

This study has important policy implications for reducing stress among investigators. Interviewees indicated that organizational changes could help alleviate stress for officers. Specifically, the interviews highlight the benefits of regularly rotating investigator assignments between units in this Criminal Investigations Section to mitigate some of the consequences of staying in a specific section for too long. For instance, paperwork burdens were widely noted by investigators in financial crimes and emotional labor was highlighted by those in child crimes. Through rotating officer assignments, it is possible to mitigate the potential consequences of investigators facing the same types of pressures for extended periods of time. Additionally, scheduling changes related to the on-call policy in the CIS made a notable difference in stress associated with working too many days in a row in this unit. Given the persistent staffing shortage in police agencies across the U.S., the necessity of overtime to fill staffing shortages, and the resulting strains on mental health, these administrative changes should be considered in other units and police agencies. The stress associated with being required to work multiple consecutive days and long hours has been linked to negative outcomes, including officer suicide in some agencies (Parrella-Aureli & Liederman, 2022). As such, the importance of identifying factors that contribute to stress, like scheduling policies that result in investigators working multiple consecutive days with no sleep, and crafting policy changes to address those factors is vital.

These findings further confirm that stress experienced by investigators is unique to their job function and differs from previously identified stressors among patrol officers. While investigators are responsible for long-term case management for specific types of cases, patrol officers provide immediate responses to a wide range of incidents before transitioning to other calls. These differences pose distinct challenges for each group. As such, identified causes of stress among patrol officers should not be generalized to investigators or other positions within a police agency. The different sources of stress between patrol officers and those assigned to specialized units should guide targeted response efforts to minimize stress among these different groups. A 'one-size-fits-all' officer wellness program that does not account for the inherently different challenges and pressures experienced by officers with different working environments is unlikely to address the unique challenges faced by all personnel within a police agency. Lastly, mental health discussions and trainings need to continue to be offered and encouraged for all members of the department, not just those serving in patrol. The negative consequences of stress can be substantial for police officers, their families, and their organizations. Ensuring that appropriate resources exist to help officers through an agency manage that stress is crucial to ensuring the health and wellbeing of the officers and the broader police organization.

Notes

1. It is important to note that the department utilized in Dabney's et al. (2013) study employed just under 2,000 officers and covered approximately 150 square miles. Further, Dabney and colleagues (Dabney et al., 2013) focused solely on homicide investigators, while the current study examined perceptions among a variety of investigators.
2. All respondents were asked all questions, except in cases where their responses guided the discussion into the topic areas without interviewer prompting. In those instances, they were asked if they had more to share related to that topic. While not examined, it is possible that respondent comfortability with being interviewed (rather than conducting interviews) and sharing information impacted interview length, resulting in shorter interviews.
3. Quotes are corrected for flow of language.

Disclosure statement

No potential conflict of interest was reported by the authors.

ORCID

Kathleen E. Padilla http://orcid.org/0000-0003-3863-2073
Jessica Huff http://orcid.org/0000-0002-8123-1470

References

Anshel, M. H. (2000). A conceptual model and implications for coping with stressful events in police work. *Criminal Justice and Behavior*, *27*(3), 375–400. https://doi.org/10.1177/0093854800027003006

Birch, P., Vickers, M. H., Galovic, S., & Kennedy, M. (2021). Cultivating well-being among police officers: Examining challenges in the workplace. In J. A. Eterno, B. Stickle, D. Scharff Peterson, & D.K. Das (Eds.), *Police behavior, hiring, and crime fighting* (pp. 3–21). Routledge.

Blue H.E.L.P. (2020). *Honoring the Service of Police Officers Who Died by Suicide*. Retrieved June 2020, from https://bluehelp.org

Brady, P. Q. (2012). *Crimes against caring: Compassion fatigue, burnout and self-care practices among professionals working with crimes against children* [Master's Thesis]. Boise State University. ScholarWorks.

Brown, J. M., & Campbell, E. A. (1990). Sources of occupational stress in the police. *Work & Stress*, *4*(4), 305–318. https://doi.org/10.1080/02678379008256993

Burns, C. M., Morley, J., Bradshaw, R., & Domene, J. (2008). The emotional impact on coping strategies employed by police teams investigating internet child exploitation. *Traumatology*, *14*(2), 20–31. https://doi.org/10.1177/1534765608319082

Carleton, R. N., Afifi, T. O., Turner, S., Taillieu, T., Duranceau, S., LeBouthillier, D. M., Sareen, J., Ricciardelli, R., MacPhee, R. S., Groll, D., Hozempa, K., Brunet, A., Weekes, J. R., Griffiths, C. T., Abrams, K. J., Jones, N. A., Beshai, S., Cramm, H. A., Dobson, K. S. . . . Asmundson, G. J. (2018). Mental disorder symptoms among public safety personnel in Canada. *The Canadian Journal of Psychiatry*, *63*(1), 54–64. https://doi.org/10.1177/0706743717723825

Collins, P. A., & Gibbs, A. C. C. (2003). Stress in police officers: A study of the origins, prevalence and severity of stress-related symptoms within a county police force. *Occupational Medicine*, *53*(4), 256–264. https://doi.org/10.1093/occmed/kqg061

Crank, J. P. (2014). *Understanding police culture*. Routledge.

Cubitt, T. I. C., & Judges, S. J. H. (2018). Show cause analysis: A qualitative assessment of the factors influencing police misconduct from the perspective of the officers who commit it. *Policing: An International Journal*, *41*(6), 782–797. https://doi.org/10.1108/PIJPSM-06-2017-0079

Dabney, D. A., Copes, H., Tewksbury, R., & Hawk-Tourtelot, S. R. (2013). A qualitative assessment of stress perceptions among members of a homicide unit. *Justice Quarterly*, *30*(5), 811–836. https://doi.org/10.1080/07418825.2011.633542

Denk-Florea, C., Gancz, B., Gomoiu, A., Ingram, M., Moreton, R., & Pollick, F. (2020). Understanding and supporting law enforcement professionals working with distressing material: Findings from a qualitative study. *Plos One*, *15*(11), 1–28. https://doi.org/10.1371/journal.pone.0242808

Eddy, A., Bergman, A. L., Kaplan, J., Goerling, R. J., & Christopher, M. S. (2021). A qualitative investigation of the experience of mindfulness training among police officers. *Journal of Police and Criminal Psychology*, *36*(1), 63–71. https://doi.org/10.1007/s11896-019-09340-7

Franke, W. D., Ramey, S. L., & Shelley, M. C. (2002). Relationship between cardiovascular disease morbidity, risk factors, and stress in a law enforcement cohort. *Journal of Occupational and Environmental Medicine*, *44*(12), 1182–1189. https://doi.org/10.1097/00043764-200212000-00014

Gershon, R. R., Barocas, B., Canton, A. N., Li, X., & Vlahov, D. (2009). Mental, physical, and behavioral outcomes associated with perceived work stress in police officers. *Criminal Justice and Behavior*, *36*(3), 275–289. https://doi.org/10.1177/0093854808330015

Gibson, C. L., Swatt, M. L., & Jolicoeur, J. R. (2001). Assessing the generality of general strain theory: The relationship among occupational stress experienced by male police officers and domestic forms of violence. *Journal of Crime and Justice*, *24*(2), 29–57. https://doi.org/10.1080/0735648X.2001.9721133

Goodison, S. E. (2022). *Local Police Department Personnel, 2020*. https://bjs.ojp.gov/library/publications/local-police-departments-personnel-2020

Henry, V. E. (1995). The police officer as survivor: Death confrontations and the police subculture. *Behavioral Sciences & the Law*, *13*(1), 93–112. https://doi.org/10.1002/bsl.2370130107

Jaramillo, F., Nixon, R., & Sams, D. (2005). The effect of law enforcement stress on organizational commitment. *Policing: An International Journal of Police Strategies & Management*, *28*(2), 321–336. https://doi.org/10.1108/13639510510597933

Krause, M. (2009). Identifying and managing stress in child pornography and child exploitation investigators. *Journal of Police and Criminal Psychology*, *24*(1), 22–29. https://doi.org/10.1007/s11896-008-9033-8

La Pelle, N. (2004). Simplifying qualitative data analysis using general purpose software tools. *Field Methods*, *16*(1), 85–108. https://doi.org/10.1177/1525822X03259227

MacEachern, A. D., Dennis, A. A., Jackson, S., & Jindal-Snape, D. (2019). Secondary traumatic stress: Prevalence and symptomology amongst detective officers investigating child protection cases. *Journal of Police and Criminal Psychology*, *34*(2), 165–174. https://doi.org/10.1007/s11896-018-9277-x

Miller, L. (2007). Police families: Stresses, syndromes, and solutions. *The American Journal of Family Therapy*, *35*(1), 21–40. https://doi.org/10.1080/01926180600698541

Nordlicht, S. (1979). Effects of stress on the police officer and family. *New York State Journal of Medicine*, *79*(3), 400–401.

The Officer Down Memorial Page (ODMP). (2016-2020). *Honoring Officers Killed in . . . [2016-2020]*. https://www.odmp.org/search/year/2020

O'hara, A. (2017, October 3). *It's Time We Talk About Police Suicide*. The Marshall Project. https://www.themarshallproject.org/2017/10/03/it-s-time-we-talk-about-police-suicide

Padilla, K. E. (2016). *Stress and maladaptive coping among police officers* [Master's Thesis]. Arizona State University. ProQuest. http://login.ezproxy1.lib.asu.edu/login?url=http://search.proquest.com/docview/1793940510?accountid=4485

Paoline, E. A., III, & Terrill, W. (2013). *Police culture: Adapting to the strains of the job*. Carolina Academic Press.

Parrella-Aureli, A., & Liederman, M. (2022, July 20). Cops in crisis: After 3 officers die of suicide in a month, colleagues say they've reached a 'breaking point'. *Block Club Chicago*. https://blockclubchicago.org/2022/07/20/cops-in-crisis-after-3-officers-die-of-suicide-in-a-month-colleagues-say-theyve-reached-a-breaking-point/.

President's Task Force on 21st Century Policing. (2015). *Final report of the President's Task Force on 21st century policing*. Office of Community Oriented Policing Services.

Rabbing, L., Bjørkelo, B., Fostervold, K. I., Strømme, H., & Lau, B. (2022). A scoping review of stress measurements and psycholemtry in police research. *Journal of Police and Criminal Psychology*, *37*(2), 457–482. https://doi.org/10.1007/s11896-022-09498-7

Roth, G. L., & Vivona, B. (2010). Mirth and murder: Crime scene investigation as a work context for examining humor applications. *Human Resource Development Review*, *9*(4), 314–322. https://doi.org/10.1177/1534484310379958

Salinas, C. R., & Webb, H. E. (2018). Occupational stress and coping mechanisms in crime scene personnel. *Occupational Medicine*, *68*(4), 239–245. https://doi.org/10.1093/occmed/kqy030

Sewell, J. D. (1994). The stress of homicide investigations. *Death Studies*, *18*(6), 565–582. https://doi.org/10.1080/07481189408252701

Simon, D. (1991). *Homicide: A year on the killing streets*. Owl Books.

Spielberger, C. D., Westberry, L. G., Grier, K. S., & Greenfield, G. (1981). *The police stress survey: Sources of stress in law enforcement*. National Institute of Justice.

Stinchcomb, J. B. (2004). Searching for stress in all the wrong places: Combating chronic organizational stressors in policing. *Police Practice & Research*, *5*(3), 259–277. https://doi.org/10.1080/156142604200227594

UCR. (2016). *2016 Crime in the United States*. https://ucr.fbi.gov/crime-in-the-u.s/2016/crime-in-the-u.s.-2016/topic-pages/violent-crime

Van Patten, I. T., & Burke, T. W. (2001). Critical incident stress and the child homicide investigator. *Homicide Studies*, *5*(2), 131–152. https://doi.org/10.1177/1088767901005002003

Violanti, J. M., & Aron, F. (1993). Sources of police stressors, job satisfaction, and psychological distress. *Psychological Reports*, *72*(3), 899–904.

Violanti, J. M., & Aron, F. (1995). Police stressors: Variations in perception among police personnel. *Journal of Criminal Justice*, *23*(3), 287–294. https://doi.org/10.1016/0047-2352(95)00012-F

Violanti, J. M., Owens, S. L., McCanlies, E., Fekedulegn, D., & Andrew, M. E. (2018). Law enforcement suicide: A review. *Policing: An International Journal*, *42*(2), 141–164. https://doi.org/10.1108/PIJPSM-05-2017-0061

OPEN ACCESS

Examining the effects of the killing of George Floyd by police in the United States on attitudes of Black Londoners: a replication

Amy Nivette, Christof Nägel and Emily Gilbert

ABSTRACT

High-profile incidents of police misconduct can have serious consequences for public trust in the police. A recent study in the *British Journal of Political Science* found that Eric Garner's death in NYC lead to more negative attitudes towards the police in London among Black residents compared to White and Asian residents. The current study aimed to replicate this transnational effect by assessing the impact of George Floyd's death on Londoners' perceptions of police. Using the same data and methodological approach, we did not replicate the immediate effect on Black Londoners' attitudes. We did find that attitudes across ethnic groups became more negative when using a wider temporal bandwidth. However, we discovered violations to the excludability assumption, meaning we cannot be certain that the effect is solely due to the murder of George Floyd, or at least partly due to different dynamics, like the effects of the COVID-19 pandemic and the accompanying policies. This means that while it is possible that police killings in other contexts play a role in shaping attitudes towards local police, these effects are difficult to disentangle from other global and local factors.

Previous research has shown that high-profile incidents of police misconduct can reduce trust and confidence in the police among the wider public (Kochel, 2019; Nägel & Lutter, 2021; Reny & Newman, 2021). However, the effects of these 'vicarious' experiences can be heterogeneous and even null depending on the institutional and societal context, sub-population, and specific circumstances of the event (Muñoz et al., 2020; Nägel & Nivette, 2022). There is relatively little research on to what extent incidents of police violence in one country resonate across the globe, influencing individual attitudes towards local police.

The study 'Phantom Pains' in the *British Journal of Political Science* aimed to address this research gap by assessing the impact of the death of Eric Garner in the United States on Londoners' attitudes towards the London Metropolitan Police in the United Kingdom (Laniyonu, 2021). His study takes advantage of the overlap between fieldwork conducted in London for the Mayor's Office for Policing and Crime [MOPAC] Public Attitude Survey and the event, utilizing the interview date as an instrumental variable to assign respondents to treatment (post-event) or control (pre-event). This type of quasi-experimental design, known as unexpected event during survey design [UESD], assumes that because the event is 'unexpected' assignment to treatment and control is as-good-as-random, conditional on a set of assumptions. Laniyonu (2021) analysed treatment effects using regression discontinuity design [RDD], and found that Black Londoners had significantly lower support for the Metropolitan Police following the death of Eric Garner. White and South Asian respondents showed little to no change following the event. Laniyonu argued that this is evidence that police violence can influence attitudes towards local police in other contexts. Specifically, he concludes that '[p]olice violence against Black persons in the US likely resonates with the experiences of Black persons in London (and elsewhere), and political actions taken in those contexts are aimed toward addressing systemic inequality there' (Laniyonu, 2021, p. 13). However, as Laniyonu (2021) rightly states, the generalizability of UESD studies is often limited due to the focus on a single case and context.

The current study aims to replicate the effect of Eric Garner's death in New York City on attitudes towards the police in London. Specifically, we conduct a replication of another high-profile event (i.e., the death of George Floyd in 2020) on attitudes towards the police using the same data from the MOPAC Public Attitude Survey in London. In addition, we evaluate the robustness and reliability of results by assessing the ignorability and excludability assumptions, as well as alternative design strategies and specifications, as recommended in the UESD literature (Muñoz et al., 2020; Nägel & Nivette, 2022). In doing so, we plan to implement the full range of 'good-practice-recommendations' discussed in the literature, thus providing a comprehensive and rigorous understanding of the hypothesized effect. The overarching goal of this replication is to critically assess the rigorousness and generalizability of causal claims regarding the transnational impact of high profile police incidents on attitudes using public opinion surveys.

The effect of police killings on attitudes towards the police

Procedural justice theory proposes that the quality of treatment and decision-making during interactions with the police can shape individual perceptions of trust and legitimacy (Mazerolle et al., 2013; Reisig et al., 2018; Solomon & Chenane, 2021; Tyler & Huo, 2002). Typically, these studies focus on direct or interpersonal interactions between an individual and a police officer. However, there is growing evidence to suggest that indirect or 'vicarious' interactions with police, such as through (social) media, can have substantive effects on attitudes towards the police (Choi, 2021; Graziano et al., 2010; Graziano, 2019; Intravia et al., 2020; Nägel & Nivette, 2022; Weitzer, 2002). In addition, these effects can be relatively greater among ethnic minority compared to majority groups, as minority group members are more likely to experience negative police contact and mistreatment (Braga et al., 2019). For example, when Michael Brown, an African American, was shot and killed by a White police officer in Ferguson, Missouri (USA), Kochel (2019) found that confidence and trustworthiness of police declined only among Black residents compared to non-Black residents. She argues that this effect was likely amplified by social identity, with African Americans 'relating more strongly to his circumstances or internalizing the experience thinking "that could have been me"' (Kochel, 2019, p. 394).

Laniyonu (2021) draws on this body of research to argue how and when incidents of police misconduct influence attitudes towards the police outside of the national context in which the incident occurred. Specifically, he outlines three explanations for why high-profile incidents in the United States could have an effect on attitudes among Afro-descendants in other contexts: 1) Afro-descendant persons maintain a shared cultural affinity and attachment, and identify with experiences of other Black individuals (Narayan, 2019; Patterson & Kelley, 2000), 2) Black residents of other countries are also more likely to experience aggressive policing tactics, such that when incidents occur in the United States, this can resonate with Black residents in particular (Bradford et al., 2009; Joseph–Salisbury et al., 2020; Millings, 2013; Vomfell & Stewart, 2021), and 3) Black residents may perceive police violence as rooted in shared experiences of racism and marginalization (Goldsmith & McLaughlin, 2022; Waters, 2014).

At the same time, Laniyonu provides several reasons why incidents in the United States may *not* have an effect on attitudes among Black residents in other countries. For example, while there may be shared identity and feelings across countries, the strength of the collective identification may differ across contexts. Police-community relations and experiences with the police may be relatively more positive among Black residents in other countries, such as Canada and the United Kingdom, compared to the United States (Laniyonu, 2021; cf. Wortley & Owusu-Bempah, 2011). The lethality of encounters with the police also differs substantially between countries. The rate of fatal police violence is higher in the US compared to England and Wales, with estimated rates of 3.418 per 1 million (2020) and 0.286 per 1 million (2019) respectively (Hirschfield, 2023). In addition, police organizations in the UK, including the Metropolitan Police, released a statement on June 3rd condemning the death of George Floyd.[1] This statement may have served as a signal to the public condemning racial injustice and reaffirming commitment to policing by consent. There are also important within-group differences in Afro-descendant attitudes towards the police, whereby Afro-Caribbean Britons have more negative perceptions of police compared to African Britons (Bradford, 2011).

In 'Phantom Pains', Laniyonu (2021) focuses on a high-profile incident of police violence in which Eric Garner died when New York City police officers restrained him lying face down on the sidewalk. On 17 July 2014, officers approached and attempted to arrest Garner for selling loose cigarettes, pinning him to the ground and placing him in a chokehold (prohibited by the NYPD). Garner stated several times that he could not breathe while pinned down before losing consciousness. He was pronounced dead about one hour later at a local hospital. Video footage captured by a bystander was released on social media soon after the event, motivating protests and the growth of the Black Lives Matter movement worldwide (Lyle & Esmail, 2016).

Based on procedural justice research and the notion of shared identity and experiences, Laniyonu (2021, p. 6) hypothesizes that 'the police killing of Eric Garner will reduce Black Londoners' evaluations of police.' Similarly, he hypothesizes that the killing of Garner will have no effect on White and South Asian Londoners' evaluations of police. Laniyonu argues, however, that the incident will only affect certain types of attitudes, specifically perceptions of fairness and satisfaction, but not effectiveness and community engagement. His third hypothesis therefore states that 'task-specific evaluations of police behavior and police work – such as effectiveness in fighting crime or engaging with the community – will be unaffected by police killings in the United States' (p. 7).

The current study

Laniyonu takes a clear approach to evaluating these hypotheses, including conducting multiple tests of relevant causal assumptions (e.g., examining non-response, pre-existing trends, simultaneous events, covariate adjustment, and examining alternative bandwidths). He shows that the results are mostly robust to these tests and alternative specifications. However, conclusions drawn from UESD studies are somewhat restricted in that they focus on a single case, limiting external validity and generalization of effects (Muñoz et al., 2020). Furthermore, recent literature on quasi-experimental designs such as UESD have emphasized the importance of checking all relevant assumptions, establishing adequate power, and evaluating the robustness of results across different model specifications (e.g., RDD and OLS, see Muñoz et al., 2020; Nägel & Nivette, 2022). For these reasons, the close evaluation of assumptions, specifications, and different case studies is necessary to determine to what extent the effect detected after an incident is robust and generalizable.

Our current study therefore aims to assess the robustness and replicability of the effect of police killings in the United States on attitudes towards the police among Black Londoners. We take Laniyonu's paper as a model for our replication, while incorporating additional tests of assumptions and alternative specifications as recommended by recent UESD literature (Muñoz et al., 2020; Nägel & Nivette, 2022). Specifically, we examine the effect of the death of George Floyd, an African American man who was killed after a White police officer knelt on his neck during a police stop on suspicion of using a counterfeit bill (BBC News, 2020b). Floyd was handcuffed, lying face down on the street, complaining of breathing difficulties. After several minutes, with the officer's knee still on his neck, Floyd became silent, and another officer could not detect a pulse. About an hour after Floyd was taken to the hospital, he was pronounced dead. The death of George Floyd sparked rapid mobilization and large-scale protests across the United States (Reny & Newman, 2021). The circumstances of Garner and Floyd's death are relatively similar, however the cases differed in the scale of media coverage following the incident. The size, scale, and broad (social) media coverage of the protests within the United States and internationally (Dunivin et al., 2022; van Haperen et al., 2022), made the George Floyd incident more likely to exert broad opinion-mobilizing effects among the public compared to relatively smaller-scale incidents and protests (Reny & Newman, 2021). Indeed, Reny and Newman (2021) show that the death of George Floyd and subsequent protests lead to less favorable views of the police across ethnic groups in the United States, but particularly among individuals with low prejudice and those identifying as politically liberal (i.e., Democrats).

Following Laniyonu (2021, pp. 6–7), we assess two hypotheses that aim to replicate the effects of the killing of George Floyd on Black Londoners' attitudes towards the police.

- H1: The police killing of George Floyd will have an effect on Black Londoners' overall evaluations (i.e., public satisfaction) and perceptions of police fairness, in comparison to White and Asian Londoners.
- H2: The police killing of George Floyd will have no effect on Black Londoners' task-specific evaluations of police behavior and work, such as police effectiveness in fighting crime or engaging with the community.

Methods

This paper has the goal to replicate the results of Laniyonu (2021) using the recent case of the death of George Floyd in 2020. The current study replicates the original UESD design, which combines observational data with natural experiments (i.e., police killings) to assign respondents to treatment (post-event) and control (pre-event). Laniyonu's study uses the MOPAC Public Attitude Survey [PAS] collected in 2014. In order to replicate the results, we use the MOPAC Public Attitude Survey [PAS] collected in 2020. The 2020 PAS contains most (but not all) of the same items used to measure the independent and dependent variables, and so we are able to replicate the original design and analysis. A list of variables included in the 2014 and 2020 PAS data is available in Appendix A. The replication was pre-registered on the Open Science Framework on 15 June 2022 (https://osf.io/tjr7a/). Any deviations from the protocol are noted below.

The code used to conduct this analysis is available on OSF (see link above). The data are available from the third author on request.

Data

The MOPAC Public Attitude Survey [PAS] is a continuous survey that conducts face-to-face interviews with a random sample of respondents across 32 London boroughs (excluding the City of London). The survey aims to complete 100 interviews in each borough per quarter, resulting in about 12,800 interviews per year. The survey covers a variety of topics surrounding perceptions of police, crime and safety, and people's experiences with crime and anti-social behavior. Prior to April 2020 and the COVID-19 pandemic, surveys were administered through Computer-Aided Personal Interviewing (CAPI), with interviewers visiting respondents in their homes. An address-based sampling approach was used, with residential addresses randomly selected from the Postcode Address File (PAF) and then a single respondent within a household randomly selected at the point of contact with the household. Following the onset of the COVID-19 pandemic, interviews were conducted via telephone in order to comply with local restrictions. Given the UK does not have a telephone sampling frame, a dual approach was used to select telephone numbers to form the sample. Firstly, a Random Digit Dialing approach was used. London-based landline telephone prefixes were auto-filled, and then random numbers were inserted in order to complete the telephone number. Secondly, a list of mobile telephone numbers known to belong to London residents who had consented to sharing their telephone number in this way was purchased from a third-party supplier. The third-party company is a commercial supplier of telephone numbers for market research and other purposes.

For both methods of data collection, the sample achieved is broadly representative of the London population across a range of demographics. Post-hoc weights are then created for each annual sample to ensure the sample reflects the London population in terms of gender, age, ethnicity, housing tenure and working status. A total of 12,736 interviews were conducted for fiscal year 2020–2021.

Power considerations

PAS is an ongoing survey that occurs year-round, with new waves beginning each fiscal year (April). The event occurred in May of 2020. For the replication analyses, we will use data collected for the fiscal year in which the event took place (i.e., 2020–2021). This ensures that the contents of the survey remain the same throughout the time period covering the event. A total of 1928 interviews were conducted prior to the event ($n = 10{,}808$ post-event). We conducted a power sensitivity analysis using G*Power to determine the minimum size of the effect that can be reliably detected using the given sample (Perugini et al., 2018). Using a two-tailed test with an alpha of 0.05 and power level of 0.80, we would be able to detect an effect size of $d = 0.069$. This suggests that we will be able to detect reasonably small effects if using the full bandwidth.

Variables

We selected variables for replication according to the original design, as reported by Laniyonu (2021), as well as additional variables to examine robustness of different scale constructions and related outcomes. Some items are only available in 2014 and not 2020 as a result of changes to the questionnaires, and so we are not able to use them in the replication. As a result, we had to deviate from the original study and pre-registration. We note these deviations below. The relevant variables for the replication include the following items from the 2020 questionnaire.

Treatment variable

The binary treatment indicator D_i will be constructed as follows:

$$D_i = \begin{cases} 0 & \text{If respondent i is interviewed before the death of George Floyd} \\ 1 & \text{If respondent i is interviewed after the death of George Floyd} \end{cases}$$

Dependent variables

In the original analysis, Laniyonu included four dependent variables: public satisfaction with police, police fairness, police effectiveness, and community engagement. The 2020 PAS did not contain the items on police effectiveness, and so we were unable to include this outcome in the analyses. In the original study, Laniyonu reconstructed the scales so that the indices range from −5 (very negative evaluation) to + 5 (very positive evaluation), with 0 reflecting neutral response values. We deviate from this approach and create a simple mean scale where outcomes range from 1 (negative evaluation) to 5 (positive evaluation). Scales were reverse-coded when necessary so that higher values equals more positive evaluations.

Public satisfaction with the police is measured using two items that ask respondents 'Taking everything into account, how good a job do you think the police in London as a whole are doing?' And 'how good a job do you think the police in your area are doing?' Note that the original analysis uses only the first item, whereas we include the second because it was available and would improve reliability.[2] Responses range from 1 'very poor' to 5 'excellent' (Cronbach's alpha = 0.77).

Police fairness was originally measured using four items, however the 2020 PAS contained only two of these four items. These asked respondents to what extent they agree with statements about police in their area (their area is defined by 15 minutes' walk from their home). The statements include: 'they [the police] can be relied on to be there when you need them,' and 'the police in your area treat everyone fairly regardless of who they are.' Respondents could indicate their agreement on a five-point Likert scale from 1 'strongly disagree' to 5 'strongly agree' (Cronbach's alpha = 0.71). The items that are not included ask whether the police are 'helpful' and 'friendly and approachable.'

Community engagement is measured using three items. Again, we were not able to include all of the items from the 2014 survey, as they were not fielded in the 2020 survey. These items asked respondents to what extent they agree that the police 'are dealing with the things that matter to people in this community,' 'listen to the concerns of local people,' and 'can be relied upon to be there when you need them.' Responses are measured on a 5-point Likert scale ranging from 1 'strongly disagree' to 5 'strongly agree' (Cronbach's alpha = 0.81). We were not able to include the original item asking whether respondents agreed that the police 'understand issues facing the local community.'

Grouping variable: ethnicity

In the original paper, ethnicity was recoded to create three groups: White, Black, and South Asian. Respondents who reported 'mixed' ethnicity (i.e., White and Black Caribbean, White and Black African) were recoded and included in the 'Black' ethnicity category.

In the 2020/2021 data, six broader categories of ethnic identity are available: Asian, Black, Mixed ethnicity, White British, White Other, and Other ethnicity.[3] We are not able to decompose the 'Mixed' category in the available data due to privacy reasons, so we exclude this category as well as 'Other ethnicity'. Note we are also not able to specify 'South Asian' respondents from the broader 'Asian' category. We will combine the White British and White Other categories to create a broader 'White' ethnicity category. As such, for the current replication, we use the following three ethnic categories: White, Black, and Asian.

Covariates

A number of covariates are included to conduct balance checks. In the original paper, Laniyonu includes: whether the respondent was stopped by the police, whether the respondent was searched or arrested, whether the respondent contacted the police, the respondent's employment status, age, and borough of residence. However, several of these covariates were not available in the 2020 PAS: whether the respondent was stopped, searched or arrested by police or has contacted the police. Our study therefore deviates slightly from the pre-registration and original study, as we are only able to include employment status, age, and borough of residence. In line with the pre-registration, we include two additional covariates in the replication: gender and whether the respondent has been a victim of crime or antisocial behaviour in the past 12 months.

Robustness and placebo checks

As an extension to the original study, we include several alternative outcomes that are in line with theoretical expectations (Sunshine & Tyler, 2003), as well as items relevant for placebo checks. The alternative outcomes include items that ask respondents to what extent they agree that 'the Metropolitan Police Service is an organisation I can trust,' whether the respondent feels 'an obligation to obey the law at all times,' and feels 'an obligation to follow police orders.' Items used for placebo checks ask to what extent the respondent agrees that the Central Government, National Health Service (NHS), and media companies are organizations that they can trust. All responses are measured on a 5-point Likert scale ranging from 1 'strongly disagree' to 5 'strongly agree.' In our pre-registration, we also planned to use the item 'The police have the same sense of right and wrong as I do,' however, it was ultimately not available in the dataset.

Analytical approach

In order to replicate the results of the original paper, we make use of the UESD identification strategy, which relies on the timing of the interview as an instrumental variable to assign respondents to control (pre-event) or treatment (post-event) groups. Because the primary objective of the proposed study is a replication of a previously published case study (Laniyonu, 2021), our design and analysis techniques resemble those used in that paper. This means we apply a regression discontinuity design which is a quasi-experimental method to analyze observational data. As part of the design, a so-called running variable is defined, which, in this case, is the day of the interview. The name-giving discontinuity results from also defining a cut-point at which a change in the level and trend of the dependent variable(s) is assumed. This cut-point is 26 May 2020, the day after George Floyd was killed by police officers in Minneapolis (likewise 17 July 2014 for Eric Garner's death). George Floyd was killed on May 25, around 8:00 AM, which corresponds to 4:00 PM London time. Since it might have taken some time for the video of the incident to spread, it is very unlikely to assume that respondents interviewed on May 25 would have been exposed to the event. Accordingly, we use May 26 as the cut-point. However, we also run robustness checks where we exclude respondents interviewed on May 25, since we cannot be entirely sure that they would belong to the control group. Respondents who were interviewed just before that day should theoretically be comparable to respondents who were interviewed just after that day, given that the interview timing is essentially as-good-as-random. Hence, all other things equal, any difference in the respective outcome (attitudinal measures of police) should be attributable to the event.

The number of days before and after the cut point (i.e., the bandwidth) is determined by a completely data-driven algorithm that approximates the smallest Mean Square Error (MSE) of the local average treatment effect (LATE). We apply both the MSE method used by Laniyonu, as well as another commonly applied procedure (Imbens & Kalyanaraman, 2012). Specifically, we replicate the 'uniform' kernel method to estimate the LATE that Laniyonu employed and extend this by the more commonly applied 'triangular' kernel approach.[4] We run models with and without covariates and with and without borough level clustered standard errors. While we use the 'rdrobust' package utilized by Laniyonu, we also run similar models with another software package, namely the 'rdd' package provided by Dimmery (2016). To explore the alleged heterogeneity of the treatment effect reported in Laniyonu, this analysis is conducted for the different ethnic groups included in the data. While we closely mirror the analysis in the Laniyonu paper, we also apply all robustness checks that are discussed in the relevant literature (Muñoz et al., 2020; Nägel & Nivette, 2022).

Specifically, we extend the RDD identification strategy by a more conventional difference-in-differences (DiD) specification in which we create the treatment variable from the product term of the respective ethnic groups and the binary event indicator. The regressions themselves are estimated by way of ordinary least squares. The hypotheses outlined above are tested by recoding the interaction of the binary event indicator with the respective ethnic groups (i.e., Black compared to all other included groups). While we base our results mainly on a model including the whole fieldwork period in order to increase statistical power, we also re-run the analysis with smaller, weekly bandwidths.

We make inferences about the effect of the death of George Floyd on perceptions of police based on p-values. We conclude that the analysis supports our hypothesis if the p-value is smaller than 0.05 using a two-tailed test. More specifically, we use heteroscedasticity-robust Huber-White standard errors (HC0) for all statistical inferences using the 'lm_robust' command from the estimator package. In order to closely replicate Laniyonu's approach, we will also apply HC2 standard errors.

Assumptions

The validity of conclusions drawn from our design hinges on two important causal inference assumptions. (1) *Excludability* implies that the timing of the interview affects the outcome through no other channel than the event itself, i.e., the exclusion restriction in instrumental variable analysis (see Labrecque & Swanson, 2018; Murray, 2006; Stock & Watson, 2007). This assumption can be violated when collateral or simultaneous events occurred unrelated time trends are present or the timing of the event itself is endogenous. We follow the literature (Muñoz et al., 2020) and apply the following robustness checks: Examination of pre-existing time trends as well as falsification tests on other units (placebo specifications for the previous year of data collection) and on other outcomes (trust in government, NHS, media) will be assessed in each case study. (2) The *ignorability* assumption addresses whether the chance of being assigned to either the control or the treatment group is as-good-as-random (Bor et al., 2014; Gangl, 2010; Legewie, 2013; Muñoz et al., 2020). Possible violations include imbalances on observables, reachability, attrition, noncompliance, heterogeneous effects. We will conduct balance tests, choose multiple bandwidth selections, adjust for covariates, and analyze non-response patterns and placebo treatments. In the pre-registration, we stated that we would conduct weekly bandwidths extending four weeks (i.e., 14, 21, 28, 35 days). Here we extend the bandwidth selection to include all possible weekly bandwidths following the event. This allows us to assess the widest possible range of effects. We provide the results of all these assumption checks in the appendix and present a brief discussion of the results in the paper.

Missing data

We use listwise deletion to restrict observations to respondents with complete information available for all covariates used in the models. We, however, do not delete observations a priori based on missing values. This way, the maximum number of observations will differ between baseline models including just the binary treatment indicator and full models including the treatment variable and covariates.

Results

Descriptive results

Table 1 summarizes the descriptive statistics of the main variables used in this analysis. The column 'mean Δ' provides the calculated difference between the group as well as a statistical test of significance (t-test) to analyze potential imbalances between groups. While all three outcome variables demonstrate significant negative differences between the treatment and the control group, the covariate distributions between respondents interviewed before and after the George Floyd incident remains largely balanced. However, the post-treatment group contains a larger number of respondents in the 35 to 44 age category, fewer respondents in the 45 to 54 age category, fewer respondents not working and more respondents who report to be unemployed. We base our results on models that include all covariates that are presented here as well as Borough level fixed effects.

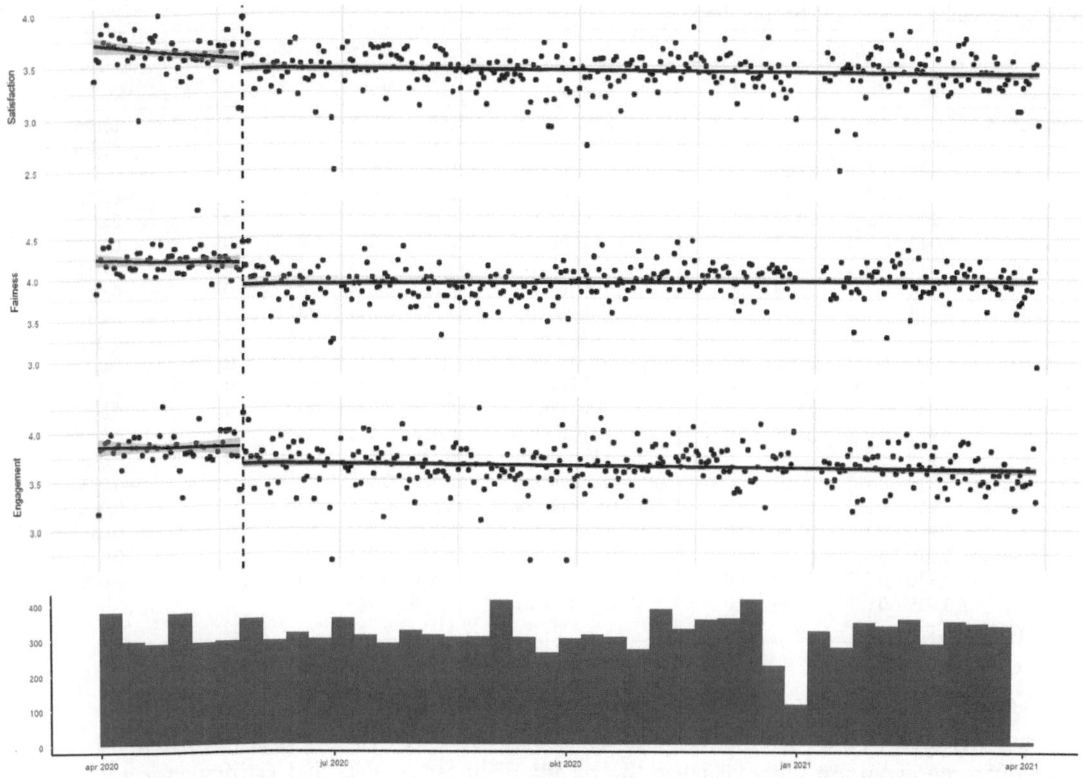

Figure 1. Outcome evolution before and after the George Floyd incident. Histograms represent daily number of interviews. Dashed line is May 25, 2020.

Simple before/after design

We extend the RDD identification strategy by a more conventional before/after specification that resembles a difference-in-differences (DiD) design, in which we create the treatment variable from the product term of the respective ethnic groups and the binary event indicator. The regressions themselves are estimated by way of ordinary least squares (OLS). The hypotheses outlined above can be tested by creating an interaction term between the binary event indicator and the respective ethnic groups (e.g., Black compared to all other included groups). Variables that were used to create the interaction were mean-centered, so that the respective main effect can be interpreted as is. In contrast to the RD models, this approach uses the entire bandwidth before and after the event (42 weeks post-event).

The results in Figure 3 indicate a negative main effect on all three outcomes. The interaction terms, however, are only significant for White respondents, showing a small positive effect. This indicates that the negative treatment effect was less pronounced for White respondents compared to Black and Asian respondents. In order to demonstrate this more clearly, we re-modelled the interaction to estimate the effect of non-white respondents (i.e., Black and Asian respondents) compared to White respondents. Figure 4 hence shows that the negative effect on all three outcomes was slightly more pronounced for non-white respondents as compared to White respondents.

Returning to our hypotheses, these findings imply that there is little evidence that attitudes changed directly after the incident (i.e., within the 2–2.5 weeks bandwidth estimated in the RDD), since the RD estimates are almost always non-significant. There is also little evidence that Black respondents' attitudes changed more negatively compared to White and Asian respondents in response to the event. While the only significant point estimates were found in the White Londoner

Table 1. Descriptive statistics and balance checks.

Control group						Treatment group							
Statistic	N	Mean	St. Dev.	Min	Max	Statistic	N	Mean	St. Dev.	Min	Max	Mean Δ	
Satisfaction	1,774	3.651	0.78	1	5	Satisfaction	9,594	3.455	0.857	1	5	−0.196	
Fairness	1,747	4.222	0.814	1	5	Fairness	9,586	3.946	0.897	1	5	−0.276	
Engagement	1,661	3.855	0.866	1	5	Engagement	9,085	3.639	0.914	1	5	−0.216	
Male	1,949	0.444	0.497	0	1	Male	10,787	0.439	0.496	0	1	−0.005	
Female	1,949	0.556	0.497	0	1	Female	10,787	0.559	0.496	0	1	0.003	
Other	1,949	0.001	0.023	0	1	Other	10,787	0.001	0.037	0	1	0	
16 to 24	1,948	0.093	0.29	0	1	16 to 24	10,787	0.078	0.268	0	1	−0.015	
25 to 34	1,948	0.226	0.418	0	1	25 to 34	10,787	0.214	0.41	0	1	−0.012	
35 to 44	1,948	0.199	0.399	0	1	35 to 44	10,787	0.234	0.424	0	1	0.035	
45 to 54	1,948	0.146	0.354	0	1	45 to 54	10,787	0.128	0.334	0	1	−0.018	
55 to 64	1,948	0.135	0.342	0	1	55 to 64	10,787	0.141	0.348	0	1	0.006	
65+	1,948	0.201	0.401	0	1	65+	10,787	0.205	0.403	0	1	0.004	
Victim	1,945	0.194	0.396	0	1	Victim	10,774	0.184	0.387	0	1	−0.01	
Fulltime	1,919	0.439	0.496	0	1	Fulltime	10,536	0.453	0.498	0	1	0.014	
Parttime	1,919	0.146	0.354	0	1	Parttime	10,536	0.147	0.354	0	1	0.001	
Not working	1,919	0.105	0.307	0	1	Not working	10,536	0.07	0.256	0	1	−0.035	***
Houseperson	1,919	0.031	0.174	0	1	Houseperson	10,536	0.026	0.16	0	1	−0.005	
Retired	1,919	0.184	0.388	0	1	Retired	10,536	0.2	0.4	0	1	0.016	
Unemployed	1,919	0.032	0.175	0	1	Unemployed	10,536	0.043	0.202	0	1	0.011	**
Student	1,919	0.043	0.203	0	1	Student	10,536	0.037	0.189	0	1	−0.006	
Other employment	1,919	0.018	0.134	0	1	Other employment	10,536	0.024	0.154	0	1	0.006	

The differences in the outcome variables can also be observed in a graphical way in Figure 1. The three outcome evolution plots visualize the results of linear models that estimate the respective outcome variables regressed on the interview date. The dashed line represents 25 May 2020; the day George Floyd was killed. There are visible but small discontinuities in the three outcome variables 'Satisfaction,' 'Fairness,' and 'Engagement.'

The histogram below the outcome evolution plots represents the daily number of interviews. As can be seen in Figure 1, the number of interviews did not change in any way before or after the incident. Accordingly, it is unlikely that the results are due to non-response patterns.

Main analysis

Regression discontinuity design

In line with our pre-registration, we first attempted to study the effect of the George Floyd incident on the attitudes of Black Londoners in a similar way to how Laniyonu investigated the effect of Eric Garner's death. Accordingly, we split the dataset by the three respective ethnic groups; Black, White, and Asian and performed a regression discontinuity analysis for each subsample with the exact same model specification according to Laniyonu's original analysis. As outlined in the pre-registration, we used 26 May 2020, as the cut-point since it might have taken some time for the video of the incident to spread, and it is very unlikely to assume that respondents interviewed on May 25 would have been exposed to the event. Results are summarized in Figure 2.

The bandwidths for satisfaction, fairness, and engagement were estimated at 18.24, 14.76, and 17.45 days, respectively. Figure 2 shows that, while the estimates are predominantly negative, none of the models show a significant difference in attitudes between the before and after comparison groups (see Appendix B for the full results). This means that we do not detect an effect on any attitudinal outcomes within the first 2 to 2.5 weeks following the incident.

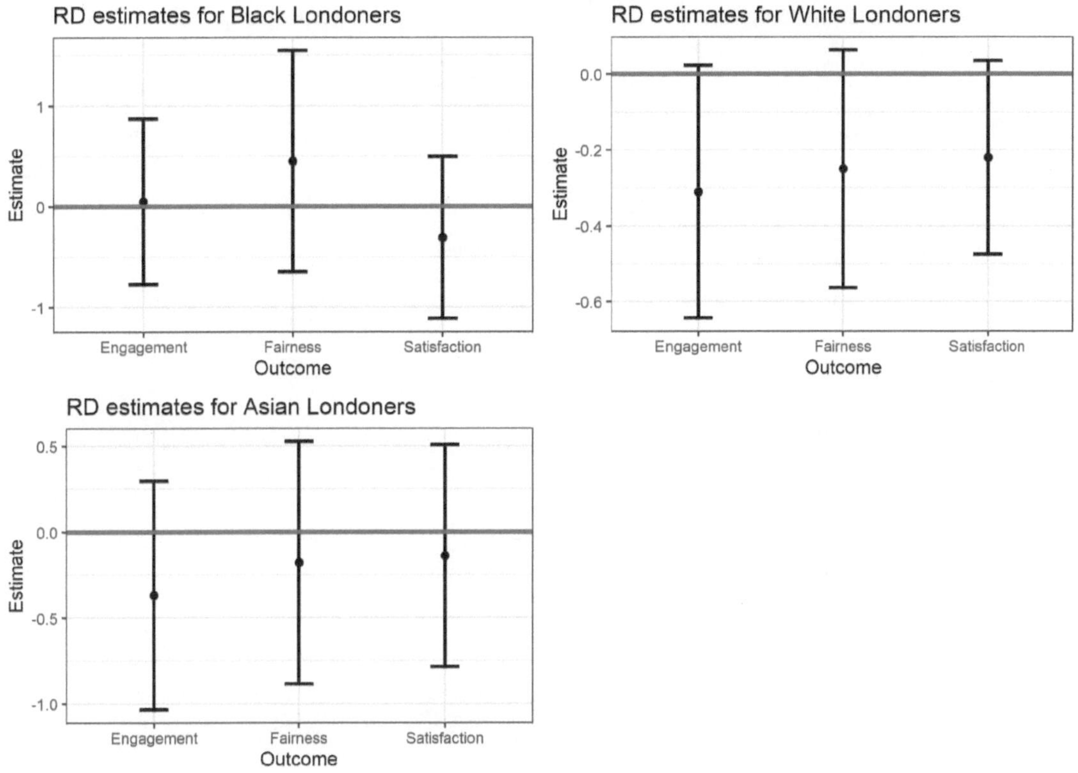

Figure 2. RD estimates and 95% confidence intervals of the effect of George Floyd's death on attitudes towards police (uniform kernel, HC2 standard errors, clustered at the borough level).

sample, we attribute this finding rather to a power issue in the other subsamples as opposed to evidence for a heterogenous treatment effect. The simple before/after comparison on the other hand, which includes the entire post-event bandwidth (42 weeks), indicates a negative effect on all three outcomes. However, there is only very limited heterogeneity in the effect sizes between ethnic groups. Thus, we do not find support for H1, since the killing of George Floyd by police did not have an effect on Black Londoners' overall evaluations (i.e., public satisfaction) and perceptions of police fairness, in comparison to White and Asian Londoners. Instead, the negative effect is ubiquitous among ethnic groups, but seemingly more pronounced for non-white respondents compared to White respondents.

In H2 we expected that the police killing of George Floyd will have no effect on Black Londoners' task-specific evaluations of police behavior and work, such as police effectiveness in fighting crime or engaging with the community. While we could not study police effectiveness since the items were not included, we found evidence that engagement was similarly affected by the incident as the other included outcome variables. Accordingly, we do not find support for this hypothesis.

Specification changes

In line with our pre-registration, we considered a number of specification changes to test the robustness of the results. These tests include: setting the cut-point to May 25 and May 27 respectively instead of May 26, (no changes to previous results except for a significant negative effect on satisfaction in the White subsample when using May 27 as cut-point, see Figures C1 and C2 in Appendix C), changing the kernel to estimate the bandwidth from 'uniform' to 'triangular' (the effect is negative and significant for engagement and satisfaction in the White Londoner sample and

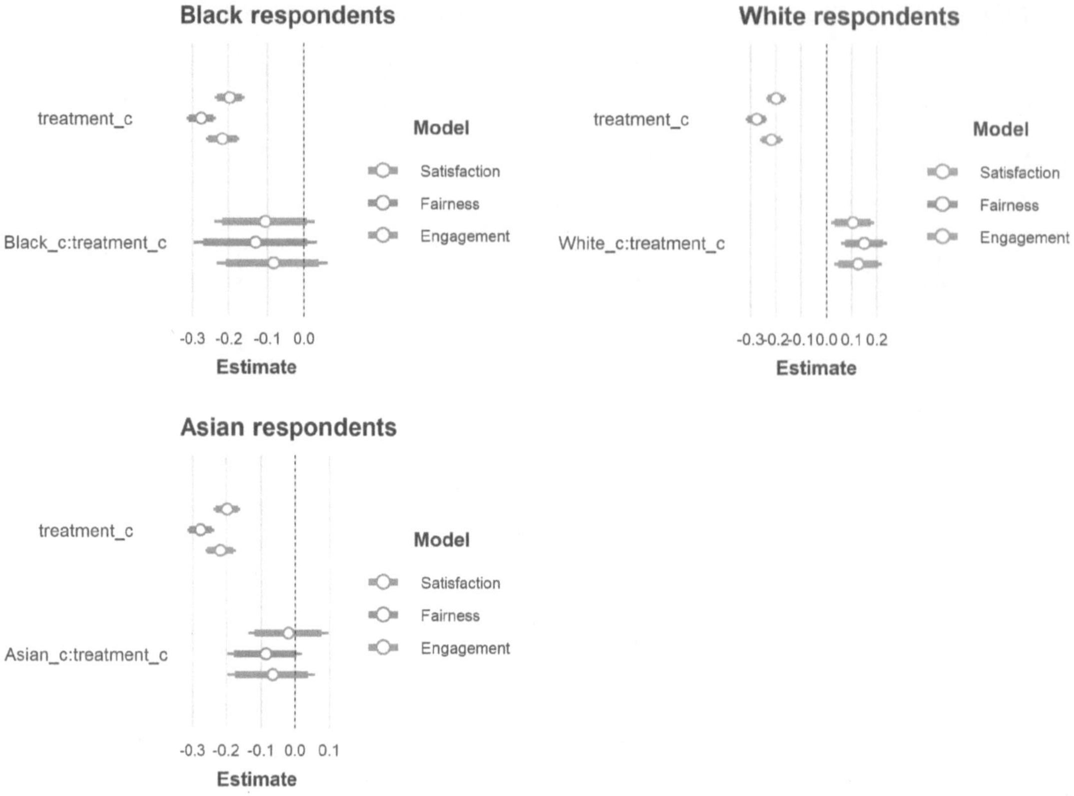

Figure 3. DiD estimates for all three ethnic groups. All covariates and borough fixed effects are included.

otherwise non-significant, Figure C3), and changing the software package to the 'rdd' package (Dimmery, 2016), which also did not alter the main results. The different RD analyses point to null or mixed results (see Figure C4). Almost all point estimates are negative but non-significant. When estimating the effect with a triangular kernel the effect becomes significant for the satisfaction and engagement outcome in the White Londoners sample. This points to the limited power when using a RD approach to identify the effect since both the triangular kernel and the White Londoner sample increase the effective sample size of the analysis. The issue of power limitations has been raised by other researchers when applying the RD approach in a political science context (Stommes et al., 2021).

Concerning the more conventional before/after specification, we pre-registered to re-run the analysis with smaller, weekly bandwidths. We decided to use all possible bandwidth choices, which resulted in 42 models for each outcome, since the fieldwork period lasted for up to 42 weeks after the George Floyd incident. We always used all respondents interviewed before the incident as the control group, and iteratively added one week to the 'treatment' group, starting with one week after the incident. Figure 5 is an attempt to visualize these $42 \times 3 = 126$ models. The picture that emerges from Figure 5 is quite clear: all estimates are significantly negative for all three outcomes when using a time window of around 2–3 weeks after the event. This points either to limited power of models using a shorter treatment window, or the notion that the negative effect of the George Floyd killing took some time to develop.

Placebo and robustness checks

We now turn to assess the robustness of the results according to the causal inference assumptions discussed in the literature (Muñoz et al., 2020). All results of the robustness and placebo checks are

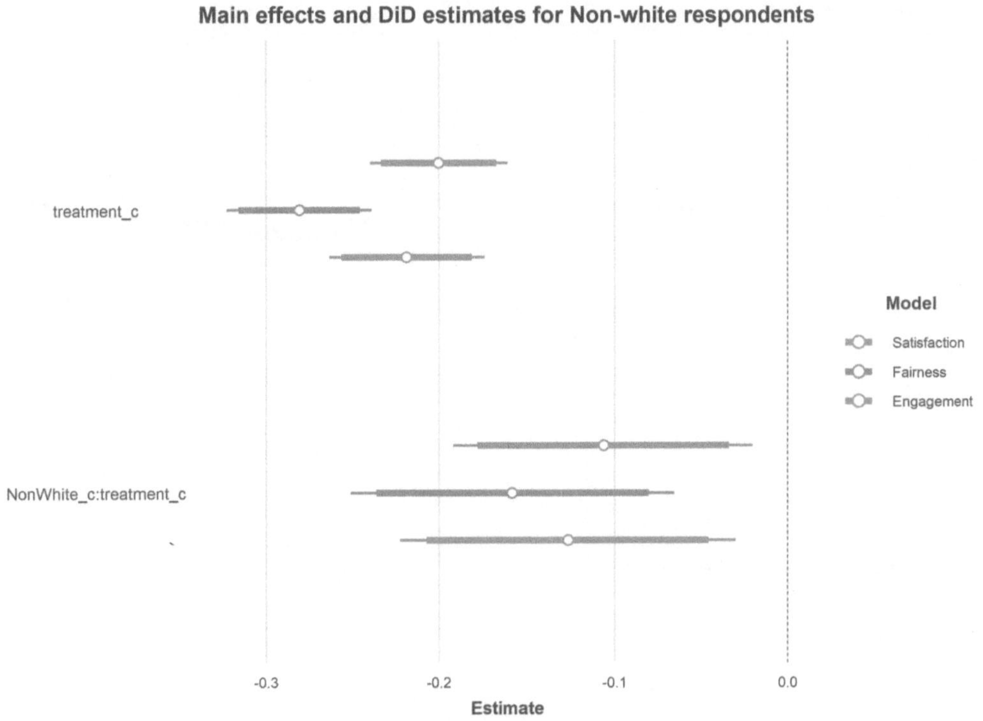

Figure 4. DiD of non-white respondents (i.e., Black and Asian respondents) compared to white respondents.

included in Appendix D. Covariate adjustment, balance checks for the complete sample, and the sensitivity of the results to the bandwidth choice have already been assessed within the previous analyses. These did not point to any violations. To further assess the validity of the ignorability assumption, we re-tested the balance for the Black subsample, inspected potential pre-existing time trends, and assessed whether there is a placebo effect when using the median of the control group as the cut-off point. Except for a slight imbalance (there less people who report to be not working in the post intervention sample), the results suggest that being assigned to the pre- or post-intervention group would not be determined by anything else than chance, i.e., according to our tests, the ignorability assumption is met.

To further investigate potential violations that relate to excludability, we checked whether there are effects of the treatment on unrelated items. Indeed, we find significant placebo effects on 'trust in the central government,' 'trust in the National Health Services,' and (although only significant for $p < 0.1$) 'trust in media companies,' which imply that the excludability assumption is violated (see Figure D4). The turbulent time in which the George Floyd incident occurred, namely the COVID-19 pandemic, might be one explanation as to why we see these placebo effects. Accordingly, our estimates are difficult to distinguish from potential spillover effects of collateral events since we cannot be entirely sure whether the effects we are identifying are solely due to our proposed treatment, i.e., the murder of George Floyd, or at least partly due to different dynamics, like the effects of the COVID-19 pandemic and the accompanying policies.

We also investigated whether we see similar effects with different survey rounds of the MOPAC Public Attitude Survey. Here, we used May 25 as the cut-point for the respective five years, from 2015 to 2019, to study whether a seasonal trend might be responsible for driving the results. As can be seen in Figure 6, there is only one significant placebo result when using 25 May 2018, as the cut-point for the fairness item. Generally, these results provide evidence that that dynamics in the outcome variable are probably not due to seasonal trends, which might bias the results.

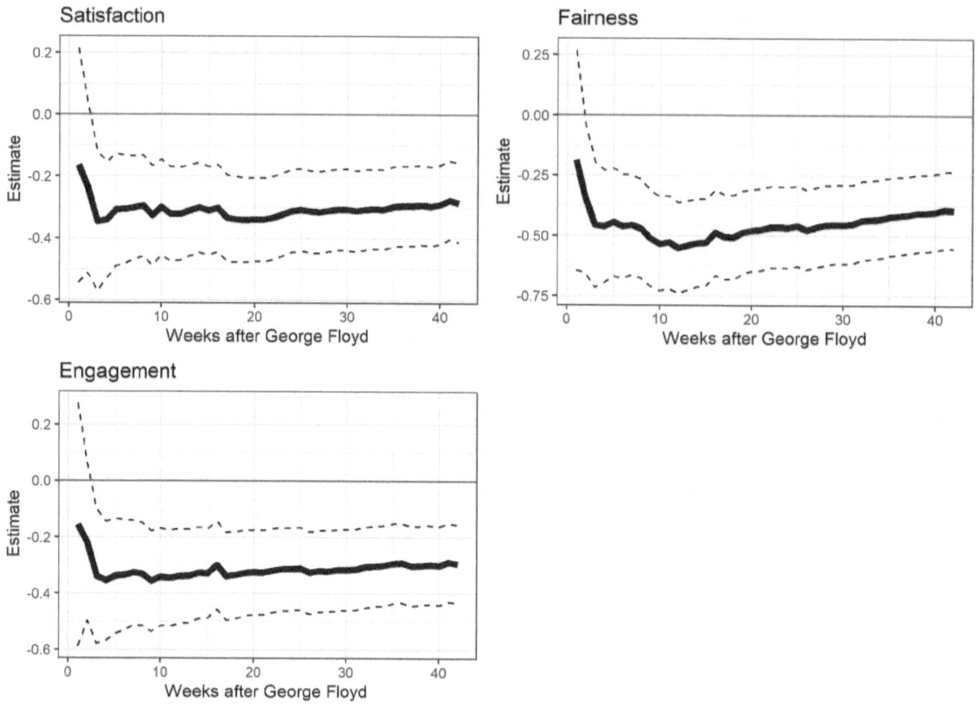

Figure 5. Point estimates and 95% confidence intervals (computed from HC0 robust standard errors) for models adding one week at a time to the 'treatment' period for the Black subsample. The control group uses the complete sample before May 25, 2020.

We also assessed the robustness of the results to using different outcome variables related to trust and police legitimacy. These include 'The Metropolitan Police Service is an organisation that I can trust,' 'I feel an obligation to obey the law at all times,' and 'I feel an obligation to follow police orders.' For all of these outcomes, we found strong negative effects (see Figure D5).

Finally, as additional analyses, we evaluate alternative cut points based on subsequent responses to the event by the Metropolitan Police and subsequent protests. This serves to examine whether Londoners were responding to the event itself, or the actions of local police. Specifically, we use RDD with the exact same specifications as in the main models (see above) to assess four additional cut points that reflect different moments in which local events and police may have shifted attitudes: 3 June (a joint statement condemning the death of George Floyd was released), 5 June (a senior Met police officer stated that the protests were unlawful and urge people not to gather in large groups), 13 June (counter-protests occur, including incidents of violence), 14 June (Metropolitan police statement condemning the violent protests and seeking a ban on further protests). The results are reported in Figure D6 in the Appendix. The results show no consistent evidence that any of these subsequent events might have had a causal impact on any of our outcomes. We do, however, find two significant effects in the Asian subgroup on both Satisfaction and Fairness with June 13 as cut point ($p < .05$). These two effects are not robust to shifting the cut point one day ahead which is why we consider these chance-findings due to running many tests. Additionally, these findings only appear in the Asian subsample and not in the Black or White subsample. It should be noted that the RDD is bound to operate with small sample sizes (in this case $n = 158$) that are close to the cut point. Non-linearities can easily be mistaken for discontinuities, which is why it is important to consider different model specifications, such as sensitivity to the chosen bandwidth and modelling of the pre- and post-slopes which might be non-linear. These two estimates are not robust to these specification changes; thus we consider them spurious.

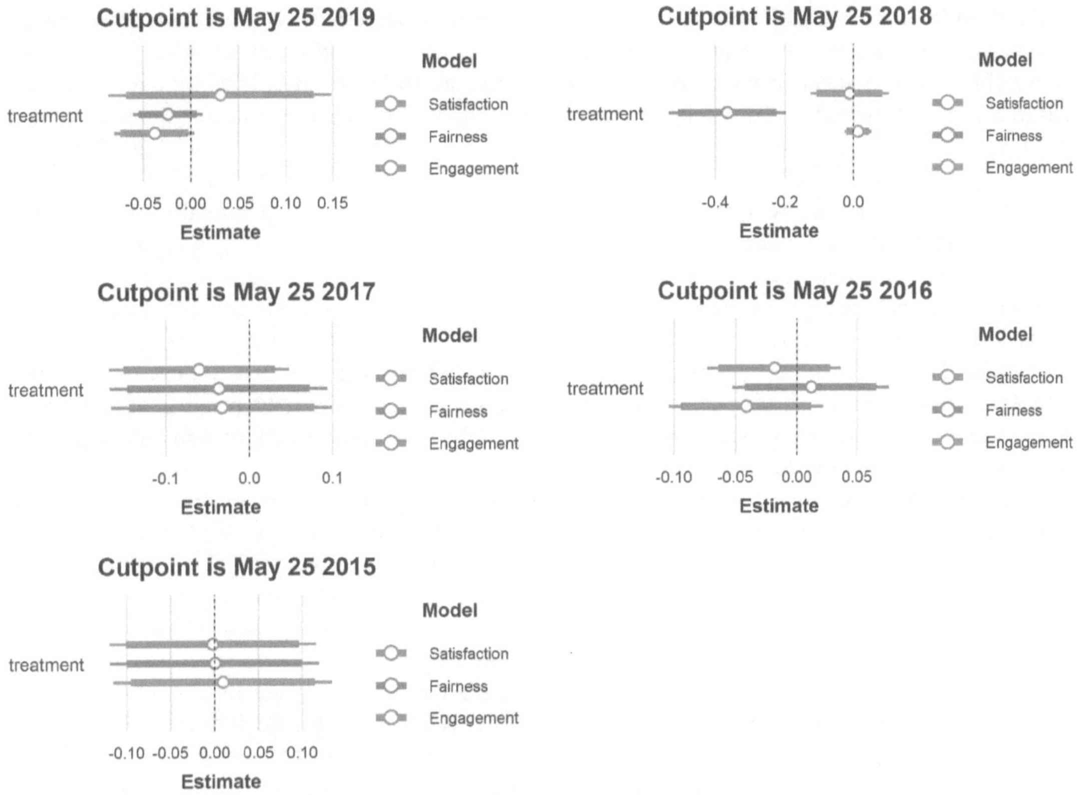

Figure 6. Placebo tests using May 25 as a cut-point in different survey years (Black subsample).

Discussion

Replication provides a tool to evaluate the generalizability and robustness of individual studies, and to what extent researchers and policymakers can be confident in certain findings (McNeeley & Warner, 2015). The current study aimed to replicate the finding that police killings in the United States can influence attitudes towards local police in other contexts. The original study found that the death of Eric Garner in the US in 2014 caused significant negative changes in evaluations of police among Black Londoners (Laniyonu, 2021). Following the original study, we used the same data source (MOPAC Public Attitude Survey), with many of the same items, and same analytical approach to examine the effect of the killing of George Floyd on Black Londoners' attitudes in 2020. Contrary to the original study, we find no immediate effects of the incident on Londoners' attitudes, regardless of ethnicity. Taking the whole time period of the survey into account, we find that attitudes were overall more negative following the death of George Floyd. There was some small heterogeneity in these effects between ethnic groups, but not in the way that was hypothesized in the original study. Black respondents did not have significantly more negative attitudes following the event compared to Asian and White respondents. Black and Asian respondents had small but significantly more negative effects compared to White respondents. One important caveat is that while we were able to establish that the ignorability assumption has not been violated, the excludability assumption was violated. This means that we cannot be certain that the death of George Floyd can exclusively account for these changes in attitudes towards police. We discuss two main implications for understanding how high-profile incidents contribute to public perceptions of police in different contexts.

First, while we were not able to reproduce the immediate effect of the incident on Black Londoners' attitudes, as demonstrated in the original study, we find evidence that the death of George Floyd was associated with overall more negative attitudes towards local police in London within a longer timeframe. This is in line with studies that show high-profile incidents of police violence can have substantive impacts on trust and police legitimacy (Kochel, 2019; Nägel & Lutter, 2021; Nägel & Nivette, 2022; Reny & Newman, 2021). However, these effects were not heterogeneous in the way that was expected based on previous research. Specifically, while Black Londoners showed more negative evaluations post-event compared to White Londoners, there was no significant difference between Black and Asian Londoners' evaluations of police following the event. This may be because the vast scope of the global media response to the murder of George Floyd led to greater exposure of the incident across population groups (Barrie, 2020; The Economist, 2020). The slightly larger effect among non-Whites suggests that the event resonated with Asian residents to a similar degree as with Black residents. This may be because of feelings of shared identity as ethnic minorities who perceive to be subject to institutional racism and aggressive policing tactics (Millings, 2013).

One can argue that media and social media scrutiny of police was more prevalent in 2020 compared to July 2014. This heightened scrutiny by the public could account for the more general effects observed following the death of George Floyd compared to Eric Garner. The death of Garner contributed to the re-ignition of the Black Lives Matter movement, which gained significant momentum following the police killing of Michael Brown in Ferguson just a few weeks after Garner's death. These high-profile incidents and subsequent protests across the US may be seen as a 'turning point' in public scrutiny of police (Capellan et al., 2020), igniting grassroots social movements calling for racial justice and police reform (Carney, 2016; Edrington & Lee, 2018). Analyses of the number of tweets including the keyword 'Black Lives Matter' show a substantial spike following the death of Michael Brown, and the volume of BLM tweets remained generally high in the years following (Giorgi et al., 2022). While BLM activism on Twitter was present prior to the death of Garner (most notably surrounding the acquittal of George Zimmerman),[5] the discourse of racial injustice and police violence on social media increased substantially and remained consistently present following Garner's and Brown's deaths. However, if higher scrutiny accounts for these effects, one would expect that we would observe more 'shocks' in public disapproval following other fatal shootings of Black individuals prior to George Floyd. In an analysis of attitudinal trends before and after the death of Floyd, Reny and Newman (2021) showed that unfavorable perceptions of police were generally declining in the period prior to the incident, which included a large number of fatal shootings (see Figure C.1, Supplemental Appendix, pg. 16). Variations in the volume and framing of media coverage, as well as the presence (or absence) of large-scale protests across different incidents may explain this heterogeneity in effects. More research is needed to understand how and why certain incidents are more likely to first gain widespread media coverage and second spark protests that mobilize public opinion.

However, it is interesting to note that the shifts in public opinion were not immediate (or detectable), as shown in the null results from regression discontinuity models. While news of the incident spread rapidly through traditional and social media outlets, large-scale public mobilization did not occur in London until a few days later on 30–31 May (Goldsmith & McLaughlin, 2022). Still, the RDD bandwidth included responses up to 2.5 weeks after the event. It is therefore likely that the subsequent protests and sustained global attention to the Black Lives Matter movement drove changes in attitudes, rather than the incident alone. With ongoing protests comes greater visibility and media coverage, and grassroots mobilization can increase public awareness of racial issues and 'activate' shifts in public opinion (Lee, 2002; Reny & Newman, 2021). As anti-racist protests continued in the weeks following George Floyd's death, police were also criticized for their handling of the protests and accused of using unlawful tactics against protesters (BBC News, 2020a; Smoke, 2020). Changes in public opinion following police violence in transnational contexts may therefore depend on whether and to what extent the incident sparks similar sustained mass mobilization, and how the police respond to protest activity.

Second, an important caveat to the above findings is that placebo tests indicated that the excludability assumption was violated. This means that while it is plausible that the death of George Floyd contributed in some way to the change in attitudes, we cannot be certain that other collateral events did not (also or entirely) play a role in this shift. The most likely collateral event at that time was the beginning of the COVID-19 pandemic and surrounding policy responses. Research suggests that the COVID-19 pandemic brought structural and racial injustice into the foreground in the United Kingdom, as the pandemic and subsequent social and financial consequences have disproportionately affected minority groups (Burgess et al., 2021; Harris et al., 2021; Katikireddi et al., 2021). Following the implementation of measures to mitigate the spread of the virus (e.g., social distancing, lockdowns, curfews), police were given expanded powers to enforce these new measures (Harris et al., 2021). While the onset of the pandemic saw 'rally' effects, leading to more positive perceptions of police and other institutions, the longer-term effects of crisis policing can deteriorate public support and cooperation (Perry et al., 2021; Sibley et al., 2020). In addition, research on policing and the pandemic in the US and UK has shown racial disparities in COVID-policing (Harris et al., 2022; Kajeepeta et al., 2022), with BLM UK declaring that racism and COVID-19 were interrelated 'deadly pandemics' (Goldsmith & McLaughlin, 2022). The effect of the death of George Floyd and subsequent protests is therefore difficult to disentangle from ongoing effects of broader institutional racism and racialized policing brought into focus by the COVID pandemic.

It is possible that other police killings at the time may be collateral events. In order to evaluate this, we take advantage of the thorough analysis conducted by Reny and Newman (2021), who examined the effect of the death of George Floyd on attitudes towards police in the US. In their robustness and mechanism checks, they examined the trends in public opinion prior to the death of Floyd that coincides with other police killings of unarmed Black individuals. In their analysis, they find that perceptions of police did not change in response to these other killings (see Figure C.1 in the Supplemental Appendix). To our knowledge, there were no police killings in the United Kingdom near the time of the event (May-June 2020). We are therefore reasonably confident that other high profile police killings did not influence the results of the current study.

In the original paper, Laniyonu (2021, p. 14) concludes that 'efforts by the Metropolitan Police to improve Black Londoners' attitudes toward the police are affected by events beyond their control.' To some extent, our results can be interpreted as support for this conclusion, as the decline does coincide with a high-profile police killing in another country and an ongoing global pandemic, which are two events that are beyond the control of local police. However, we hesitate to come to the same conclusion for two reasons. First, the presence of several collateral events means that we cannot be entirely sure which factor, or combination of factors, contributed to these changes. Second, it is possible that attitudes changed as a result of how local police responded to these events. Most notably, the expanded police powers and enforcement of COVID restrictions may have played an important role in contributing to declining satisfaction with the police during this period (Ghaemmaghami et al., 2022; Perry et al., 2021). Indeed, the slight delay in effect suggests that attitudes may be responding to how the local police *reacted* to the protests instead of (or in addition to) the event and protests themselves.

Nevertheless, research suggests that these events mobilize opinion because they resonate with *local* historical and lived experiences of structural and institutional inequality. This implies that any reforms must address both embedded structural inequalities and improve accountability, transparency, and reconciliation in policing (Bell, 2017; Goldsmith & McLaughlin, 2022). For example, Bell (2017) argues that democratization of the police is one important step in reducing inequalities and building community trust. In particular, openly providing information on interactions and body worn cameras can help improve transparency, and ultimately build trust: 'If one suspects that most police interactions go the way they should, data and transparency can potentially be a boon to solidarity between officers and communities. Data can perhaps put what police actually do most of the time in clearer perspective' (Bell, 2017, pg. 2144). Minimizing the likelihood of disproportionate and deadly use of force is also imperative to prevent these incidents from occurring in the first place. An evaluation of police use of deadly force in the United States found that agencies that required officers to file a report for any incident in which they pointed their gun but did not shoot had significantly lower rates of fatal shootings by police compared to agencies that did not require this (Jennings & Rubado, 2017). The authors argue that this requirement may have led officers to use more caution when using their weapon, and signal an institutional commitment to minimizing unnecessary use of force. Training in de-escalation tactics, especially involving unarmed and erratic citizens, may also help to reduce unnecessary use of force incidents (Engel et al., 2022). However, more research is needed to understand the processes in which police use force, how the use of force is distributed across encounters, and identify the sources of racial disparities in the use of force (Bennell et al., 2021).

Limitations and conclusion

We highlight several limitations to this replication study. First, while we were able to use the same ongoing survey to replicate the measures and test the effect, not all items that were fielded in 2014 were available in the 2020 PAS. Notably, we were not able to test the null effect of the event on the task-specific evaluation of police effectiveness as Laniyonu hypothesized. We suspect that, given the wider placebo effects we detected, that we may have also found negative overall effects stemming from experiences with COVID policing. However, this is speculation, and more research is needed to understand how personal and vicarious experiences of injustice differentially impact affective and instrumental evaluations of police. Second, another notable difference from the original is the composition of our ethnic group categories. Due to privacy issues, we were not able to disaggregate the 'mixed' category, which may include respondents with Afro-Caribbean and African backgrounds. Without these individuals in the analysis, lose power and may have underestimated the size of the treatment effect. Third, while we have discussed the implications of the COVID pandemic on estimating causal effects, it is still important to note that the pandemic serves as an important difference between the original context and our replication. In addition, researchers have noted that the wider opinion-mobilizing effects of the death of George Floyd were in part the result of a cumulation of frustration and amplification following multiple deaths of Black Americans by police (Reny & Newman, 2021). This makes the comparison between Eric Garner and George Floyd similar in circumstance but embedded in different social and political contexts. These differences in context may in part explain why we were not able to replicate the results of the original study.

Nevertheless, replication serves as one important step in the accumulation of knowledge about how vicarious experiences influence national and international public opinion. A single study or replication tells only part of the story, and so does a single replication. Systematic reviews and meta-analyses are needed to summarize effects and evaluate conditions that lead to heterogeneity (Lösel, 2018). Although the current study did not replicate the original results, we found that it is plausible that police killings in other contexts, alongside other global and local factors, can influence attitudes towards local police. However, the presence of collateral events and violation of the exclusion restriction means that we cannot be certain which factor(s) contributed to overall changes in attitudes towards police in London. Future research should continue examine when and how these incidents lead to widespread media coverage, spark protests, and influence attitudes towards local police across the globe.

Notes

1. See: https://news.npcc.police.uk/releases/uk-police-stand-with-those-appalled-by-george-floyd-death.
2. These two items are generally referred to as measures of 'confidence', however Laniyonu (2021) refers to the item as 'satisfaction'. We use the term 'satisfaction' instead of confidence in order to maintain consistency with the original paper. In addition, we ran models using only the single item in line with Laniyonu's analysis, and results were unchanged.
3. The White and White Other background includes English, Welsh, Scottish, Northern Irish, British, Irish, Gypsy or Irish Traveller, and Any other White background. The Asian or Asian British category includes Indian, Pakistan, Bangladeshi, Chinese, and Any other Asian background. The Black category includes African, Caribbean, and any other Black/African/Caribbean background. The Mixed category includes White and Black Caribbean, White and Black African, White and Asian, and Any other mixed/multiple ethnic backgrounds. The Other ethnic group includes Arab and Any other ethnic group.
4. The triangular kernel method uses a local linear regression (LOESS) and gives observations closer to the cut point more weight. The uniform kernel on the other hand weights all observation equally.
5. George Zimmerman fatally shot Trayvon Martin, an unarmed 17 year old African American student, on February 26, 2012. Zimmerman claimed he acted in self-defense. On July 13, 2013, Zimmerman was acquitted of murder and manslaughter charges.

Disclosure statement

No potential conflict of interest was reported by the authors.

Funding

The work was supported by the Nederlandse Organisatie voor Wetenschappelijk Onderzoek [VI.Vidi.191.135].

ORCID

Amy Nivette http://orcid.org/0000-0003-0597-3648
Christof Nägel http://orcid.org/0000-0003-2161-539X

References

Barrie, C. (2020). Searching racism after George Floyd. *Socius: Sociological Research for a Dynamic World*, *6*, 237802312097150. https://doi.org/10.1177/2378023120971507

BBC News. (2020a, June 7). George Floyd: London anti-racism protests leave 27 officers hurt. *BBC News*. https://www.bbc.com/news/uk-england-london-52954899

BBC News. (2020b, July 16). George Floyd: What happened in the final moments of his life. *BBC News*. https://www.bbc.com/news/world-us-canada-52861726

Bell, M. C. (2017). Police reform and the dismantling of legal estrangement. *The Yale Law Journal*, *126*(7), 2054–2150.

Bennell, C., Alpert, G., Andersen, J. P., Arpaia, J., Huhta, J., Kahn, K. B., Khanizadeh, A., McCarthy, M., McLean, K., Mitchell, R. J., Nieuwenhuys, A., Palmer, A., & White, M. D. (2021). Advancing police use of force research and practice: Urgent issues and prospects. *Legal and Criminological Psychology*, *26*(2), 121–144. https://doi.org/10.1111/lcrp.12191

Bor, J., Moscoe, E., Mutevedzi, P., Newell, M. -L., & Bärnighausen, T. (2014). Regression discontinuity designs in epidemiology: Causal inference without randomized trials. *Epidemiology*, *25*(5), 729–737. https://doi.org/10.1097/EDE.0000000000000138

Bradford, B. (2011). Convergence, Not Divergence?: Trends and trajectories in public contact and confidence in the police. *The British Journal of Criminology*, *51*(1), 179–200. https://doi.org/10.1093/bjc/azq078

Bradford, B., Jackson, J., & Stanko, E. A. (2009). Contact and confidence: Revisiting the impact of public encounters with the police. *Policing and Society*, *19*(1), 20–46. https://doi.org/10.1080/10439460802457594

Braga, A. A., Brunson, R. K., & Drakulich, K. M. (2019). Race, place, and effective policing. *Annual Review of Sociology*, *45*(1), 535–555. https://doi.org/10.1146/annurev-soc-073018-022541

Burgess, R. A., Kanu, N., Matthews, T., Mukotekwa, O., Smith-Gul, A., Yusuf, I., Lamptey, I., Macauley, N., Wilson, R., Pirisola, M., & Gul, M. (2021). Exploring experiences and impact of the COVID-19 pandemic on young racially minoritised people in the United Kingdom: A qualitative study. *PLoS One*, *17*(5), e0266504. https://doi.org/10.1371/journal.pone.0266504

Capellan, J. A., Lautenschlager, R., & Silva, J. R. (2020). Deconstructing the Ferguson effect: A multilevel mediation analysis of public scrutiny, de-policing, and crime. *Journal of Crime and Justice*, *43*(2), 125–144. https://doi.org/10.1080/0735648X.2019.1652921

Carney, N. (2016). All lives matter, but so does race: Black lives matter and the evolving role of social media. *Humanity & Society*, *40*(2), 180–199. https://doi.org/10.1177/0160597616643868

Choi, J. (2021). Asymmetry in media effects on perceptions of police: An analysis using a within-subjects design experiment. *Police Practice & Research*, *22*(1), 557–573. https://doi.org/10.1080/15614263.2020.1749624

Dimmery, D. (2016). https://cran.r-project.org/web/packages/rdd/index.html

Dunivin, Z. O., Yan, H. Y., Ince, J., & Rojas, F. (2022). Black lives matter protests shift public discourse. *Proceedings of the National Academy of Sciences*, *119*(10), e2117320119. https://doi.org/10.1073/pnas.2117320119

Edrington, C. L., & Lee, N. (2018). Tweeting a social movement: Black lives matter and its use of twitter to share information, build community, and promote action. *Journal of Public Interest Communications*, *2*(2), 289. https://doi.org/10.32473/jpic.v2.i2.p289

Engel, R. S., Corsaro, N., Isaza, G. T., & McManus, H. D. (2022). Assessing the impact of de□escalation training on police behavior: Reducing police use of force in the Louisville, KY metro police department. *Criminology & Public Policy*, *21*(2), 199–233. https://doi.org/10.1111/1745-9133.12574

Gangl, M. (2010). Causal Inference in Sociological Research. *Annual Review of Sociology*, *36*(1), 21–47. https://doi.org/10.1146/annurev.soc.012809.102702

Ghaemmaghami, A., Inkpen, R., Charman, S., Ilett, C., Bennett, S., Smith, P., & Newiss, G. (2022). Responding to the public during a pandemic: perceptions of 'satisfactory' and 'unsatisfactory' policing. *Policing: A Journal of Policy and Practice*, *15*(4), 2310–2328. https://doi.org/10.1093/police/paab058

Giorgi, S., Guntuku, S. C., Himelein-Wachowiak, M., Kwarteng, A., Hwang, S., Rahman, M., & Curtis, B. (2022). *Twitter corpus of the #blacklivesmatter movement and counter protests: 2013 to 2021*. arXiv:2009.00596). arXiv. https://doi.org/10.1609/icwsm.v16i1.19373

Goldsmith, A., & McLaughlin, E. (2022). Policing's new vulnerability re-envisioning local accountability in an era of global outrage. *The British Journal of Criminology*, *62*(3), 716–733. https://doi.org/10.1093/bjc/azab073

Graziano, L. M. (2019). News media and perceptions of police: A state-of-the-art-review. *Policing: An International Journal*, *42*(2), 209–225. https://doi.org/10.1108/PIJPSM-11-2017-0134

Graziano, L. M., Schuck, A., & Martin, C. (2010). Police misconduct, media coverage, and public perceptions of racial profiling: An experiment. *Justice Quarterly*, *27*(1), 52–76. https://doi.org/10.1080/07418820902763046

Harris, S., Joseph-Salisbury, R., Williams, P., & White, L. (2021). *A collision of crises: Racism, policing, and the COVID-19 pandemic*. Runnymede Trust, Centre on the Dynamics of Ethnicity. May. https://www.runnymedetrust.org/publications/collision-of-crises-racism-policing-and-the-covid-19-pandemic

Harris, S., Joseph-Salisbury, R., Williams, P., & White, L. (2022). Notes on policing, racism and the Covid-19 pandemic in the UK. *Race & Class*, *63*(3), 92–102. https://doi.org/10.1177/03063968211063436

Hirschfield, P. J. (2023). Exceptionally Lethal: American police killings in a comparative perspective. *Annual Review of Criminology*, *6*(1). annurev-criminol-030421-040247. https://doi.org/10.1146/annurev-criminol-030421-040247.

Imbens, G., & Kalyanaraman, K. (2012). Optimal bandwidth choice for the regression discontinuity estimator. *The Review of Economic Studies*, *79*(3), 933–959. https://doi.org/10.1093/restud/rdr043

Intravia, J., Thompson, A. J., & Pickett, J. T. (2020). Net legitimacy: Internet and social media exposure and attitudes toward the police. *Sociological Spectrum*, *40*(1), 58–80. https://doi.org/10.1080/02732173.2020.1720554

Jennings, J. T., & Rubado, M. E. (2017). Preventing the use of deadly force: The relationship between police agency policies and rates of officer-involved gun deaths. *Public Administration Review*, *77*(2), 217–226. https://doi.org/10.1111/puar.12738

Joseph-Salisbury, R., Connelly, L., & Wangari-Jones, P. (2020). "The UK is not innocent": Black lives matter, policing and abolition in the UK. *Equality, Diversity and Inclusion: An International Journal, 40*(1), 21–28. https://doi.org/10.1108/EDI-06-2020-0170

Kajeepeta, S., Bruzelius, E., Ho, J. Z., & Prins, S. J. (2022). Policing the pandemic: Estimating spatial and racialized inequities in New York City police enforcement of COVID-19 mandates. *Critical Public Health, 32*(1), 56–67. https://doi.org/10.1080/09581596.2021.1987387

Katikireddi, S. V., Lal, S., Carrol, E. D., Niedzwiedz, C. L., Khunti, K., Dundas, R., Diderichsen, F., & Barr, B. (2021). Unequal impact of the COVID-19 crisis on minority ethnic groups: A framework for understanding and addressing inequalities. *Journal of Epidemiology and Community Health, 75*(10), 970–974. https://doi.org/10.1136/jech-2020-216061

Kochel, T. R. (2019). Explaining racial differences in ferguson's impact on local residents' trust and perceived legitimacy: Policy implications for police. *Criminal Justice Policy Review, 30*(3), 374–405. https://doi.org/10.1177/0887403416684923

Labrecque, J., & Swanson, S. A. (2018). Understanding the assumptions underlying instrumental variable analyses: A brief review of falsification strategies and related tools. *Current Epidemiology Reports, 5*(3), 214–220. https://doi.org/10.1007/s40471-018-0152-1

Laniyonu, A. (2021). Phantom pains: The effect of police killings of black Americans on black British attitudes. *British Journal of Political Science, 52*(4), 1–17. https://doi.org/10.1017/S0007123421000557

Lee, T. (2002). *Mobilizing public opinion: Black insurgency and racial attitudes in the civil rights era*. University of Chicago Press.

Legewie, J. (2013). Terrorist events and attitudes toward Immigrants: A natural experiment. *The American Journal of Sociology, 118*(5), 1199–1245. https://doi.org/10.1086/669605

Lösel, F. (2018). Evidence comes by replication, but needs differentiation: The reproducibility issue in science and its relevance for criminology. *Journal of Experimental Criminology, 14*(3), 257–278. https://doi.org/10.1007/s11292-017-9297-z

Lyle, P., & Esmail, A. M. (2016). Sworn to protect: Police brutality – a dilemma for america's police. *Race, Gender & Class, 23*(3–4), 155–185.

Mazerolle, L., Antrobus, E., Bennett, S., & Tyler, T. R. (2013). Shaping citizen perceptions of police legitimacy: A randomized field trial of procedural justice: Shaping citizen perceptions of police. *Criminology, 51*(1), 33–63. https://doi.org/10.1111/j.1745-9125.2012.00289.x

McNeeley, S., & Warner, J. J. (2015). Replication in criminology: A necessary practice. *European Journal of Criminology, 12*(5), 581–597. https://doi.org/10.1177/1477370815578197

Millings, M. (2013). Policing British Asian Identities: The enduring role of the police in Young British Asian Men's situated negotiation of identity and belonging. *The British Journal of Criminology, 53*(6), 1075–1092. https://doi.org/10.1093/bjc/azt041

Muñoz, J., Falcó-Gimeno, A., & Hernández, E. (2020). Unexpected event during survey design: Promise and pitfalls for causal inference. *Political Analysis, 28*(2), 186–206. https://doi.org/10.1017/pan.2019.27

Murray, M. P. (2006). Avoiding invalid instruments and coping with weak instruments. *Journal of Economic Perspectives, 20*(4), 111–132. https://doi.org/10.1257/jep.20.4.111

Nägel, C., & Lutter, M. (2021). The 2017 French riots and trust in the police: A quasi-experimental approach. *European Journal of Criminology, 20*(1), 22. https://doi.org/10.1177/1477370821998974

Nägel, C., & Nivette, A. E. (2022). Unexpected events during survey design and trust in the police: A systematic review. *Journal of Experimental Criminology*. https://doi.org/10.1007/s11292-022-09508-y

Narayan, J. (2019). British black power: The anti-imperialism of political blackness and the problem of nativist socialism. *The Sociological Review, 67*(5), 945–967. https://doi.org/10.1177/0038026119845550

Patterson, T. R., & Kelley, R. D. G. (2000). Unfinished migrations: Reflections on the African diaspora and the making of the modern world. *African Studies Review, 43*(1), 11. https://doi.org/10.2307/524719

Perry, G., Jonathan-Zamir, T., & Factor, R. (2021). The long-term effects of policing the COVID-19 pandemic: Public attitudes toward the police in the 'new normal. *Policing: A Journal of Policy and Practice, 14*(4), 1073–1091. https://doi.org/10.1093/police/paab070

Perugini, M., Gallucci, M., & Costantini, G. (2018). A practical primer to power analysis for simple experimental designs. *International Review of Social Psychology, 31*(1), 20. https://doi.org/10.5334/irsp.181

Reisig, M. D., Mays, R. D., & Telep, C. W. (2018). The effects of procedural injustice during police–citizen encounters: A factorial vignette study. *Journal of Experimental Criminology, 14*(1), 49–58. https://doi.org/10.1007/s11292-017-9307-1

Reny, T. T., & Newman, B. J. (2021). The opinion-mobilizing effect of social protest against police violence: Evidence from the 2020 George Floyd Protests. *The American Political Science Review, 115*(4), 1–9. https://doi.org/10.1017/S0003055421000460

Sibley, C. G., Greaves, L. M., Satherley, N., Wilson, M. S., Overall, N. C., Lee, C. H. J., Milojev, P., Bulbulia, J., Osborne, D., Milfont, T. L., Houkamau, C. A., Duck, I. M., Vickers-Jones, R., & Barlow, F. K. (2020). Effects of the

COVID-19 pandemic and nationwide lockdown on trust, attitudes toward government, and well-being. *The American Psychologist*, *75*(5), 618–630. https://doi.org/10.1037/amp0000662

Smoke, B. C. (2020, June 9). Police accused of unlawful tactics at London BLM Protests. *Vice News*. https://www.vice.com/en/article/pkypnz/police-accused-of-unlawful-tactics-at-london-blm-protests

Solomon, S. J., & Chenane, J. L. (2021). Testing the fair process heuristic in a traffic stop context: Evidence from a factorial study with video vignettes. *The British Journal of Criminology*, *61*(4), 1086–1106. https://doi.org/10.1093/bjc/azaa096

Stock, J. H., & Watson, M. W. (2007). *Introduction to econometrics* (2. ed., Pearson international ed.). Pearson Addison-Wesley.

Stommes, D., Aronow, P. M., & Sävje, F. (2021). On the reliability of published findings using the regression discontinuity design in political science. *ArXiv:2109.14526 [Stat]*. http://arxiv.org/abs/2109.14526

Sunshine, J., & Tyler, T. R. (2003). The role of procedural justice and legitimacy in shaping public support for policing. *Law Society Review*, *37*(3), 513–548. https://doi.org/10.1111/1540-5893.3703002

The Economist. (2020, June 9). George Floyd is remembered around the world. *The Economist*. https://www.economist.com/graphic-detail/2020/06/09/george-floyd-is-remembered-around-the-world

Tyler, T. R., & Huo, Y. J. (2002). *Trust in the Law: Encouraging public cooperation with the police and courts*. Russell Sage Foundation.

van Haperen, S., Uitermark, J., & Nicholls, W. (2022). The Swarm versus the grassroots: Places and networks of supporters and opponents of black lives matter on twitter. *Social Movement Studies*, *22*(2), 1–19. https://doi.org/10.1080/14742837.2022.2031954

Vomfell, L., & Stewart, N. (2021). Officer bias, over-patrolling and ethnic disparities in stop and search. *Nature Human Behaviour*, *5*(5), 566–575. https://doi.org/10.1038/s41562-020-01029-w

Waters, R. (2014). African Canadian anti-discrimination activism and the transnational civil rights movement, 1945–1965. *Journal of the Canadian Historical Association*, *24*(2), 386–424. https://doi.org/10.7202/1025083ar

Weitzer, R. (2002). Incidents of police misconduct and public opinion. *Journal of Criminal Justice*, *30*(5), 397–408. https://doi.org/10.1016/S0047-2352(02)00150-2

Wortley, S., & Owusu-Bempah, A. (2011). The usual suspects: Police stop and search practices in Canada. *Policing and Society*, *21*(4), 395–407. https://doi.org/10.1080/10439463.2011.610198

How generalizable are findings from police surveys? A review of multi-agency studies

Erin M. Kearns and Justin Nix

ABSTRACT
Policing scholars frequently use surveys to understand officer attitudes and behavioral intentions. Yet, it is difficult to gain access to one – let alone multiple – agencies. Thus, officer surveys often reflect views in a single department, making it unclear how generalizable the findings are. For the present study, we conducted an exploratory review of articles published in 16 criminology and policing journals from 2000 to 2017. We identified 600 studies that involved surveying one or more samples of police officers. From this list, we set out to determine: (1) how often authors administered their surveys to more than one sample, and (2) when surveys were administered to more than one sample, how often were results consistent across samples? We found eighty-seven (14.5%) articles that involved collecting survey data from multiple agencies, though only 29 (4.8% overall, 33.3% of multi-agencies studies) met our inclusion criteria. Importantly, only 15 studies could be analyzed as some authors no longer had data, could not share data, or did not response to our emails. Results were fully consistent across samples in just one published study. In the other studies, findings partially replicated – though sometimes results were in the opposite direction across departments. Thus, replication is critical before policy is created from single-agency surveys.

Introduction

In the last few decades, policing scholars have increasingly used survey research methods to understand officers' perceptions and attitudes (Nix et al., 2019). For example, through officer surveys, researchers have gained a better understanding of what motivates people to pursue a career in policing (White et al., 2010), how officers view their agency once they have started working (Wolfe & Nix, 2017), and perceptions of support seeking and willingness to engage mental health service among law enforcement officers (Karaffa & Koch, 2016; Lambert & Steinke, 2015). Similarly, scholars have examined variation in officer perceptions of policing crime types including traffic violations (Bates et al., 2015), sexual assault (Wentz & Archbold, 2012), terrorism (Kearns, 2020; Muibu, 2022), and interpersonal violence (Gracia et al., 2014). Further, amidst tense relationships between law enforcement and the public – particularly over the last decade – policing survey studies have provided insights on officer views on topics including citizen review (Lee et al., 2017), community policing (Kearns, 2017), use of force (Ingram et al., 2014), de-policing (Nix et al., 2018), and body-worn cameras (Gaub et al., 2016).

Studies using officer surveys certainly contribute to what we know about policing. Yet, it often remains unknown how generalizable findings are to other agencies. To collect data from officers in any given department, researchers need the chief's permission. The reality, unfortunately, is that it is often difficult to gain access to one – let alone multiple – agencies. Police can be distrustful of academics and may not see the benefit of participating in their research (Reiner, 2000; Skogan, 2015). As a result, it has become quite common for scholars to publish their findings from surveys administered to single agencies. Complicating matters, there is growing consensus across multiple disciplines that replication is vital to the scientific endeavor (Murayama et al., 2014). Yet, replication is rare in criminology and criminal justice – with replication studies making up between 0.45% (Pridemore et al., 2018) and 2.34% of published articles (McNeeley & Warner, 2015).

Presumably scholars shy away from replications studies because they are more difficult to publish. For example, Galiani et al. (2017, p. 2) found that 'In a survey of editors, almost all responded they would in principle publish a replication study that overturned the results of the original study, but only 29% responded that they would consider publishing a replication study that confirmed the original study results.' This is problematic with over 17,000 state and local law enforcement agencies of various sizes, geographies, populations served, political landscapes, et cetera in the United States where – presumably – what matters in a major police department on the East Coast might not translate to a small-town department in the Midwest. Such heterogeneity might result in 'hidden moderators' (see e.g., Van Bavel et al., 2016; c.f. Inbar, 2016; Olsson-Collentine et al., 2020) preventing results from a study of one agency from fully replicating in a separate study of any other agency. Indeed, it is well-documented that police organizations can influence the subculture – and the behaviors – of the officers they employ (Chan, 1996; Crank, 1990; Fyfe, 1988; White, 2001; Wilson, 1968). Accordingly, the unknown generalizability of single-agency surveys deserves more attention than a throwaway 'limitation' line in the discussion section.

We endeavored to accomplish the following in our exploratory study: (1) identify the percentage of studies using police surveys published between 2000 and 2017 that collected data from more than one department and (2) identify how often the results were consistent across the agencies among the studies that did include multiple departments. First, we outline the importance of replication in criminology and criminal justice research – particularly that on policing and officer perceptions. We next describe the sample frame, data, coding, and analytical approach. Finally, we conclude with a discussion of the findings and their limitations, policy implications stemming from these findings, and future research directions.

Background

Particularly over the last decade, the 'open science movement' has pushed to make scientific research more transparent and accessible within scientific communities and across broader society. Amidst this, organizations like the Center for Open Science have been created with the mission to 'increase openness, integrity, and reproducibility of research.'[1] One core tenant of reproducible scientific research is that scholars can and should *replicate* their studies. The push to replicate social science research is nothing new. Nearly 30 years ago, Gary King (1995) called for replication in political science with his recommendations on how the field – from faculty and students to funders and editors – could incentivize and implement this process. More recently, psychology has faced a so-called 'replication crisis' as the field grappled with canonical papers failing to replicate and what that meant for the discipline (Bohannon, 2015; Francis, 2012; Maxwell et al., 2015; Shrout & Rodgers, 2018).

As Pridemore et al. (2018) note, criminology has yet to face the same challenges to our knowledge bases through systematic or larger scale replications. In a more extensive look at the literature, Pridemore et al. (2018) found that only 0.45% of published articles in criminology were replication studies – a far smaller percentage than the 2.34% that McNeeley and Warner (2015) reported. Notably, three quarters of these replications were successful and another 15% produced mixed results, which is promising for the future of replication work in criminology and criminal justice. Further, replication has received more attention within the field over the last handful of years. For example, key points from a session on replication at the 2017 American Society of Criminology annual meeting now appear in the *Journal of Experimental Criminology* (Farrington et al., 2019), the *Journal of Contemporary Criminal Justice* published a special issue on replication in 2018 (Savolainen & VanEseltine, 2018), and *Police Practice and Research* is currently publishing a special issue on replication within policing studies.

Amidst the increasing emphasis on replication, David Weisburd (in Farrington et al., 2019, p. 388) noted that 'replication is important to science because it improves our ability to define the impacts of programs or practices. But it is a mistake to begin with the idea that the replications will bring us certainty.' Within the field, some areas of study may be more likely to produce replicable findings due to the nature of data available, methodological control, homogeneity of groups being studied, and relative stability in societal and cultural precursors over time. However, as both Robert Boruch and Friederich Lösel (in Farrington et al., 2019) state, there are numerous cultural, societal, political, temporal, and other changes over time that make it unlikely that findings will replicate over time and place. It is reasonable to expect that this may be particularly the case for policing survey research given: a) the influence that organizational culture can have on officer attitudes and behaviors (Shupard & Kearns, 2019; Silver et al., 2017), b) the mandate for police to be responsive to the unique needs of the community they serve; and c) the sheer heterogeneity in size, geography, demographics, et cetera across law enforcement agencies.

Blaskovits et al. (2018) aimed to conduct a full replication of Telep and Lum's (2014) examination of U.S. police officers' receptivity to empirical research using a Canadian sample. Findings across these two studies were similar in several ways, though Blaskovits et al. (2018) sample also indicated greater openness to evidence-based policing. This singular example of a full replication attempt within policing survey research is encouraging. However, more attempts to replicate policing survey research are certainly needed to better understand whether the similar findings across agencies is a broader trend, limited to certain topics or issues, or a more anomalous finding. The current study aims to answer this question by identifying how often survey results were consistent across multiple agencies among studies published between 2000 and 2017 in 15 criminology and policing journals.

Methods

Sampling frame and data

To begin, we adopted Nix et al. (2019) sampling frame that included a total of 16 journals – eight policing-focused journals and eight prestigious general criminology and criminal justice journals. We searched the eight policing-focused journals listed on the American Society of Criminology's Division of Policing website (https://ascpolicing.org/members-corner/): *European Journal of Policing Studies, International Journal of Police Science & Management, Journal of Police and Criminal Psychology, Police Practice & Research, Police Quarterly, Policing & Society, Policing: A Journal of Police and Practice*, and *Policing: An International Journal.* We also searched eight prestigious general criminology journals (see Nix et al., 2019 for a full discussion): *British Journal of Criminology, Crime & Delinquency, Criminal Justice and Behavior, Criminology, Journal of Criminal Justice, Journal of Quantitative Criminology, Journal of Research in Crime and Delinquency*, and *Justice Quarterly*. As Nix et al. (2019) noted, online access to *European Journal of Policing Studies* was not available and thus they excluded this journal from their study. For the present study, we were able to find abstracts for all 127 articles published in the journal between 2012 and 2017 but could not find full text of many of the articles; thus, we also excluded this journal from our study.

Our first inclusion criterion was that studies involved survey data collection from police officers. We searched each of these journals for articles using survey data from police officers that were published between 2000 and 2017 (including 'online first'). We identified 600 articles that met this criterion. Our next inclusion criterion was that the study collected data from multiple departments, which eliminated most studies, leaving 87 (14.5% of total).

For our analytic sample, we focused on articles where comparisons of officer survey data was both logical and feasible. First, given cross-national variation in policing practices and organizational structures, we excluded articles ($n = 14$) where data were collected from officers in different countries. Second, several studies used samples of officers across many departments with only a small number of officers in any one department participating. Since department-level samples could not be identified in these cases, these studies were excluded from our sample ($n = 11$). Third, a few studies did systematically sample from multiple departments, but the sample sizes in at least one of the departments was too small for department-specific comparisons to be sufficiently powered. Thus, between-department comparisons were not statistically feasible, so these studies were also excluded ($n = 10$). Finally, many policing studies come from the Project on Policing Neighborhoods (POPN) data which includes officer interviews and ethnographic observations. We excluded POPN studies wherein the variables come from a source other than surveys, since survey data is the focus of this project ($n = 23$). In sum, we only included studies where: a) data came from officer surveys, including experimental, cross-sectional, and panel data, b) the researcher(s) systematically sampled officers in at least two departments, c) departments were in the same country, and d) department-specific analyses were feasible and sufficiently powered. See Figure 1 for a flow chart summarizing our sampling approach and exclusion criteria.

Taking all the above into account, our final analytic sample is comprised of the 29 studies (4.8% of total; 33.3% of studies including multiple departments) that met our inclusion criteria across articles published in these journals between 2000 and 2017. Table 1 presents each of the journals included in this study and – for each journal – the number of articles published in each between 2000 and 2017 that surveyed police officers (criterion 1), the number of those articles that surveyed officers in multiple departments (criterion 2), and the number of articles that met all our inclusion criteria and thus were in the final sample.

Procedure

Once we identified the 29 studies that met our inclusion criteria, each of the present authors separately reviewed each study to determine whether it provided sufficient data to compare results across departments. Seven (24.1%) of the published manuscripts did provide sufficient information for us to compare findings across departments while 22 (75.9%) did not. We next contacted the corresponding author for each of these 22 manuscripts via email to request the results disaggregated by department.[2] The body of those emails was as follows:

> Hi Dr. {insert corresponding author's last name here},
>
> A colleague and I are examining studies that have collected survey data from officers in multiple police departments. Your study [TITLE] in [JOURNAL] is one of the articles that we would like to include. If possible, could you provide us with [INSERT WHAT IS NEEDED FROM THIS STUDY]? Please accept my apologies if I missed this information in the text.
>
> Thanks! [Erin Kearns & Justin Nix]

Of the 22 authors whom we contacted, eight provided the data that we requested, 10 responded that they either no longer had the data or had agreed not to disaggregate it as a condition of IRB or department participation, and four did not respond to our initial or follow up email. Thus, we were able to compare the replicability of findings across departments for 15 studies (2.5% of total; 17.2% of studies on multiple departments; 51.7% of studies that meet our inclusion criteria).

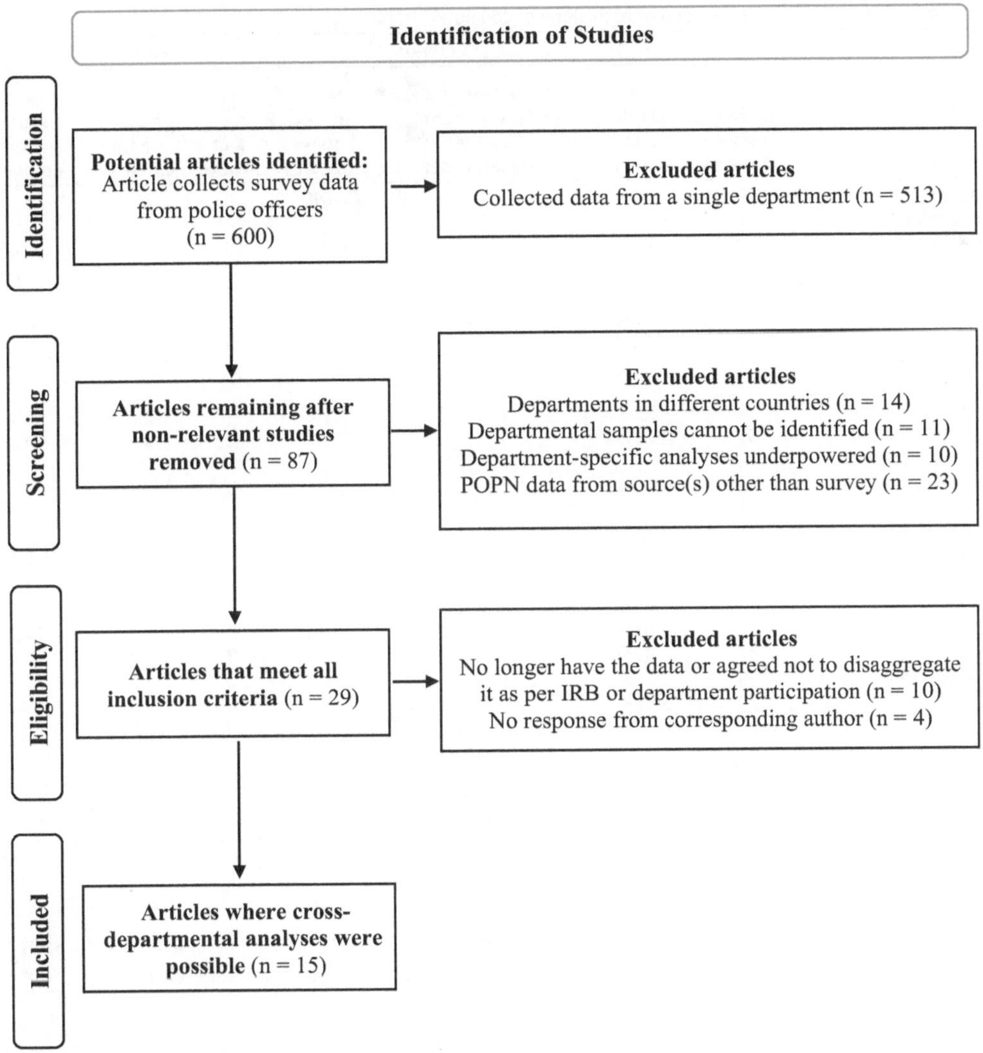

Figure 1. Article identification flow diagram.

Analytic plan

After we either disaggregated each study's results based on information in the published manuscript or received disaggregated results from the study's corresponding author, we then identified four main components of each study. First, we identified the research question(s) for each study. Second, we noted key aspects of each sample including: the number of departments, the sample size for each department, the response rate, and any notable similarities or differences described across departments. Third, we identified the dependent and independent variables in each study. Finally, where findings were disaggregated by department, we examined if each result was a) consistent in significance & direction, b) inconsistent in significance only, or c) inconsistent in significance & direction. We then compared the findings to see where there are consistencies or inconsistencies – essentially examining the replicability of findings across agencies within a single study.

Full replication materials for the tables and figures in the present manuscript will be posted on the authors' websites upon publication. We will also post full replication materials for two of the 15

Table 1. List of journal and articles included at each stage of coding.

	Criterion 1		Criterion 2		Final Sample		
	# of Articles using Surveys	% of all Articles using Surveys	# of Articles using Surveys from Multiple Departments	% of Articles from Criterion 1	# of Articles	% of Articles from Criterion 1	% of Articles from Criterion 2
British Journal of Criminology	6	1.0%	0	0.0%	0	0.0%	—
Crime & Delinquency	18	3.0%	5	27.8%	3	16.7%	60.0%
Criminal Justice and Behavior	24	4.0%	2	8.3%	0	0.0%	0.0%
Criminology	8	1.3%	6	75.0%	0	0.0%	0.0%
International Journal of Police Science & Management	69	11.5%	3	4.3%	0	0.0%	0.0%
Journal of Criminal Justice	37	6.2%	3	8.1%	1	2.7%	33.3%
Journal of Police and Criminal Psychology	55	9.2%	3	5.5%	2	3.6%	66.7%
Journal of Quantitative Criminology	0	0.0%	0	—	0	—	—
Journal of Research in Crime and Delinquency	2	0.3%	2	100%	0	0.0%	0.0%
Justice Quarterly	16	2.7%	9	56.3%	3	18.8%	33.3%
Police Practice & Research	59	9.8%	6	10.2%	2	3.4%	33.3%
Police Quarterly	87	14.5%	14	16.1%	8	9.2%	57.1%
Policing & Society	40	6.7%	6	15.0%	3	7.5%	50.0%
Policing: A Journal of Police and Practice	27	4.5%	1	3.7%	0	0.0%	0.0%
Policing: An International Journal	152	25.3%	27	17.8%	7	4.6%	25.9%
TOTAL ARTICLES	600	100%	87	14.5%	29	4.8%	33.3%

studies analyzed here , (Kearns, 2017; Nix et al., 2017) but we do not have permission to share the original replication materials for the other 13 articles analyzed in this manuscript.

Results

The main objective of this study was to examine the prevalence of consistent findings in surveys of police officers across departments. Of the 600 published studies using surveys of police that we identified, few ($n = 87$; 14.5%) collected data from officers in multiple departments. Even fewer studies ($n = 29$; 4.8%) systematically collected officer-level data across multiple departments with samples large enough to compare statistically.

As shown in Figure 2, there has been an increase in the number of articles published using officer surveys over time – with a particular uptick in 2016 and 2017 – across the 18 years in our sample. In the years immediately preceding this, community-police relations were widely and hotly debated in the aftermath of high-profile incidents where police used deadly force against unarmed Black citizens across the United States (Nix et al., 2018), and concurrently, there were marked decreases in public confidence in police.[3] During the same period, President Obama convened the Task Force on 21st Century Policing (Ramsey & Robinson, 2015) and body-worn cameras were being increasingly adopted by law enforcement agencies around the country (see Jennings et al., 2014) among other shifts. Thus, the increased academic focus on understanding how police view the communities they serve, their responsibilities and changes to them, their departments, and other aspects of policing logically follows. Of note, however, is that a similar uptick in the percentage of studies that surveyed multiple agencies does not occur during this same time.

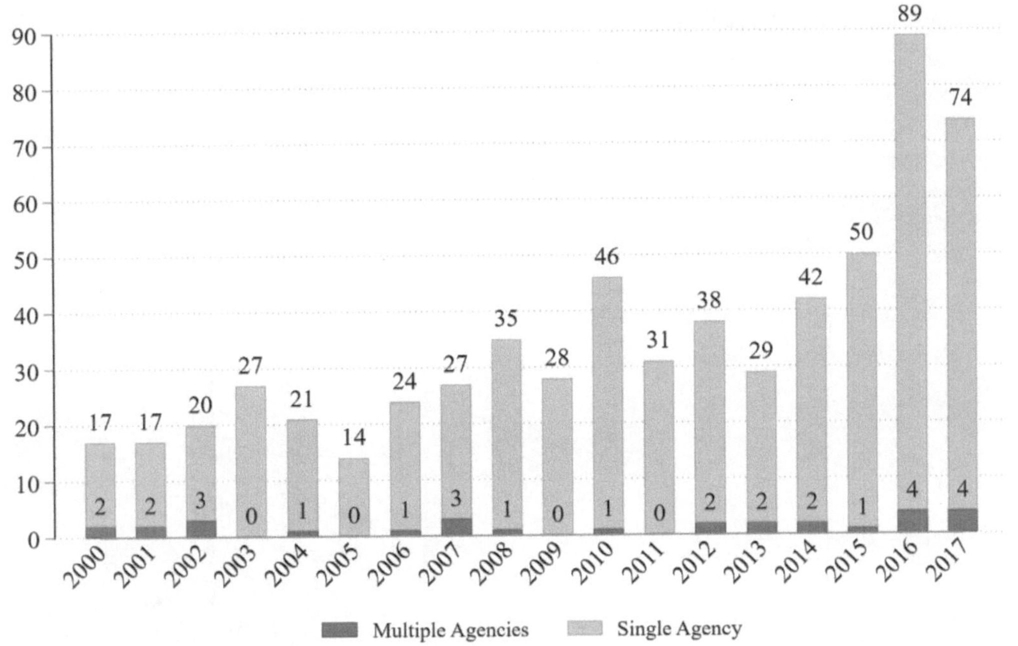

Figure 2. Number of officer survey articles published per year 2000–2017. Note: Multiple agency articles refer to the 29 articles that meet the inclusion criteria for this study.

In Figure 3, we disaggregate by journal the number of articles published in each 2-year interval using a single versus multiple agencies. There are notable differences in the frequency that research on officer attitudes and behavioral intentions have been published across the 15 journals in our sample – seven of which are policing-focused and eight of which are general criminology and criminal justice journals. Perhaps unsurprisingly, most articles using officer survey data – regardless of whether a single agency or multiple agencies were included – have been published in policing-focused journals (end of second row and full third row). In policing-focused journals, there appears to be some variation in frequency of publishing officer survey papers both by outlet and over time. Across more general criminology and criminal justice focused journals, however, there seems to be more between-outlet variation than temporal. See the online Table A1 for the underlying data used to create Figure 3.

As Table 2 shows, there were 15 studies that met our inclusion criteria and that we could also either examine between-department differences based on the published results or the authors provided us with supplemental analyses upon request. Table 2 notes the topic of the study, number of departments surveyed, the sample sizes for each department, the range of response rates across departments, a brief description of the similarities and differences between departments, and how consistent the findings were across departments. Each of the 15 articles surveyed between two and four ($M = 2.67$; $SD=0.82$) agencies. Broadly, most of the studies can be grouped into studying one of the following four topics: views on evidence-based policing, intelligence-led policing, police misconduct, or police culture. At the department-level, sample sizes ranged from $N = 59$ to 523 ($M =$ 199.85; $SD=125.13$) and response rates ranged from 7.3% to 98.5%.

Across the 15 survey-based studies of police officers in multiple agencies where between-department comparisons are possible, the analytic strategies vary both in the statistical techniques used and the number of analyses conducted. For example, one study presents only descriptive statistics (Telep & Lum, 2014) while another presents only exploratory factor analysis (Domingues & Machado, 2017). One includes ranking variables alongside mean comparisons (Westmarland & Rowe, 2018), while others present means comparisons across numerous variables (Darroch &

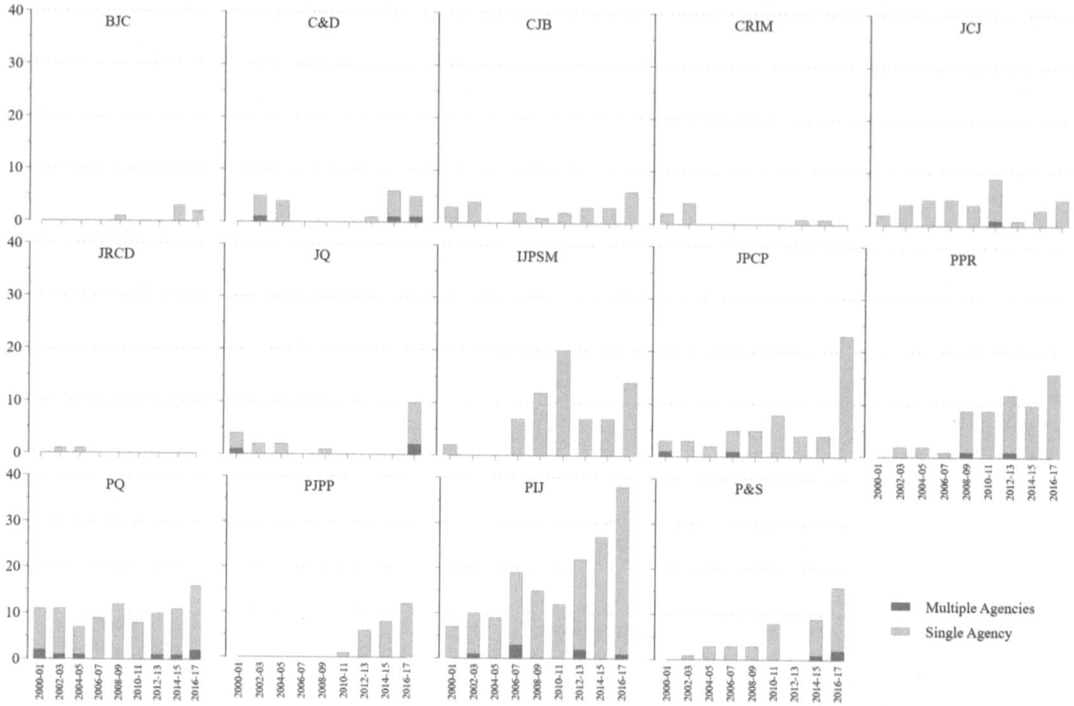

Figure 3. Number of officer survey articles published per 2-year increments by journal 2000–2017. Notes: Multiple agency articles refer to the 29 articles that meet the inclusion criteria for this study. *Journal of Quantitative Criminology* did not publish any articles using officer surveys between 2000 and 2017.

Mazerolle, 2015; Ivkovich & Khechumyan, 2013; Paoline, 2004; Sherwood, 2000), and others still rely primarily (Paoline et al., 2000) – or solely – upon regression (Chu & Sun, 2014; Darroch & Mazerolle, 2013; Gaub et al., 2016; Kearns, 2017; Nix et al., 2017; Sun & Chu, 2008; Telep, 2017). Accordingly, it is challenging to simply answer 'how often do results replicate?' To address this, the far-right column of Table 2 notes each study's analytical approach and succinctly summarizes between-department comparisons of findings.

As shown in Table 2, results only completely replicated in one study (#15) which conducted exploratory factor analysis in two departments. Domingues and Machado (2017) surveyed officers in two departments to examine sources of officers' stress. Using exploratory factor analysis where data were both pooled and then disaggregated by department, the same three-factor model was suggested with similar factor loadings. In another study (#10), the findings nearly replicate fully. Nix et al. (2017) administered a survey experiment in two agencies to test the causal effects of suspect demeanor on police officers' willingness to use procedural justice. In both departments, officers indicated it was less important to treat disrespectful suspects with procedural fairness. However, whereas the authors used just one measure of demeanor in their first survey (disrespect), in the second survey they included separate measures for verbal and symbolic disrespect – with only the latter significantly reducing officers' perceived importance of using procedural justice.

Six studies rely solely (#4, #5, #8, #10, #11) or partially (#12) on regression analyses. Five of the six studies have at least one coefficient that is significant in the same direction across departments while one fails to replicate a single result across departments. All six studies also have coefficients that are in the same direction, even if they are statistically significant in some departments but not others. Further, in most (83.3%) of these studies, at least one of the coefficients is also significant in multiple departments but in opposite directions. One study (#1) presented descriptive information about pre- and post-deployment attitudes toward body worn cameras and compared percent

Table 2. Replicability of findings across multiple departments.

		Sampling				
Article	Research Area	# Depts	N	RR	Dept. Notes	Replicability of Findings
1	Perceptions of body worn cameras	3	106, 153, 205	77% – 92%	2 close, 1 different	Descriptive & percent change comparisons. Pre- and post-deployment officers in Phoenix were more negative about BWCs than officers in either Spokane or Tempe. Pre to post attitudes comparisons across departments show consistent significance & direction, same direction but not all significant, and significant in opposite direction
2	Familiarity with evidence-based policing	3	523, 343, 94	36% – 78%	2 states, 2 capitals	Descriptive analyses. Similar findings across departments, though smaller rural agency scored higher in some areas.
3	Relative uptake of intelligence-led policing	4	67, 75, 59, 85	70% – 82%	Strong v. weak innovation	Mean comparisons. No difference between strong uptake sites on some outcomes and differences on others. No differences regardless of innovation level on some outcomes as well.
4	Receptivity to evidence-based policing	4	523, 276, 71, 122	38% – 77.5%	Diverse in size of force, jurisdiction & geography	Regression models. Coefficients a mix of consistent in significance & direction and consistent in direction but not all significant.
5	Domestic violence views by gender	2	159, 113	88.3% – 95.6%	2 largest cities in Taiwan	Regression models. None of the independent variables have a significant relationship with the dependent variable in both departments, though there is some consistency in non-significant independent variables.
6	Perceptions of police misconduct	3	102, 110, 308	7.3% – 41.1%	2 large cities w/rural parts & 1 small rural in different areas	Ranking offense seriousness nearly consistent across agencies. Mean likelihood of reporting varies by officer's rank and agency.
7	Uptake of intelligence-led policing innovation	4	67, 75, 59, 86	70.3% –82.4%	Strong v. weak innovation	Mean comparisons. No differences on some variables. Significant differences on other variables though no consistently lower agency.
8	Views on policing by gender	2	206, 130	>90% - >95%	2 largest cities in Taiwan	Regression models. Coefficients a mix of consistent in significance & direction and consistent in direction but not all significant.
9	Perceptions of police misconduct	2	232, 236	79% – 88%	Large capital v. rural, more junior force	Mean comparisons. Mostly similar views on rule violations & seriousness. Capital force indicated greater willingness to report and punish offenses.
10	Perceptions of procedural justice, race, and demeanor	2	242, 251	20% – 70%	2 Southeastern cities: 1 large, half white; 1 mid-sized, majority white	Regression models. Coefficients a mix of consistent in significance & direction and consistent in direction but not all significant.
11	Support for community policing with minorities	3	417, 135, 161	94.9% – 98.5%	All in DC metro area, varied size & % rural	Regression models. Coefficients a mix of consistent in significance & direction and consistent in direction but not all significant.

(*Continued*)

Table 2. (Continued).

		Sampling				
Article	Research Area	# Depts	N	RR	Dept. Notes	Replicability of Findings
12	Views that are part of 'police culture' as per conventional wisdom	2	398, 240	93% – 98%	Both near national average for % of minority and female officers	Mean comparisons. No difference on some variables. Significant differences on other variables though no consistently lower agency. Regression models. Coefficients a mix of consistent in significance & direction, consistent in direction but not all significant, and significant in opposite directions.
13	Enrichment of the policing job	2	171, 243	42.4% – 47.7%	Both urban; smaller one also more decentralized	Mean comparisons. Significant differences between departments on most core job characteristics. Differences by rank vary between departments. Largely no differences by education in either department.
14	Views on boundaries of occupational culture of police	2	398, 240	93% – 98%	Both near national average for % of minority and female officers	Mean comparisons. Between-agency differences on some variables but not others, though no consistently lower agency. Direction of correlates for each cluster the same for each agency, though not always same significance.
15	Sources of officers' organization stress	2	210, 303	Not listed	One dept was younger, had fewer years of exercise, and fewer members	EFA. In both departments, a three-factor model is suggested with the same three factors and similar factor loadings.

change in those attitudes, which varied across the three departments. Another study (#2) presented descriptive analyses, which are largely similar across departments though one agency scored higher in some areas. In study (#6), officers were asked to rank the seriousness of offenses, which is largely consistent across agencies. This study was also one of the seven (along with #3, #7, #9, #12, #13, #14) that used between-department mean comparisons across variables. In each of these studies, there were significant between-department differences for some variables but not others. Sometimes one agency had consistently different views, other times this was not the case.

In sum, the authors of these 15 studies more often than not found that at least some of their results replicated across departments. Very few police survey studies collect data from multiple departments and even fewer do so systematically and with large enough samples to compare findings between departments. Across the 15 studies where between-department comparisons of results were possible, only one study replicated completely while another nearly replicated fully. Findings replicated partially for most of the other studies, though sometimes results were significant in the opposite direction. Finally, one study failed to replicate a single significant finding across departments.

Discussion

At the onset of this project, we aimed to first identify the percentage of studies using police surveys published between 2000 and 2017 that collected data from more than one department and then identify how often the results were consistent across the agencies among the studies that did include multiple departments. Overall, a relatively small percentage (14.5%) of the published articles collected data from multiple departments where replication would be possible. However, for nearly half of these articles, there was not enough information in the text for us to disaggregate the analyses ourselves and the author(s) were unable to provide those analyses or did not respond to our email request. While Blaskovits et al.'s (2018) replication of Telep and Lum (2014) was promising, only two of the 15 articles in our final analytic sample showed a similar degree of replication. Though results were mixed for most of the other studies – and there is reason to believe that replication may be lower in policing studies given the influence of organizational culture (Paoline, 2021) – this does highlight the need for both better reporting on articles that are published to enable future studies such as the present one and more replication efforts such as Blaskovits et al. (2018).

With the 'open science movement' and emphasis on replication across social science disciplines (King, 1995; Simons, 2014), it is certainly time to take seriously how criminology and criminal justice will address these topics. We are still at the early stages of our disciplinary discussions on replication (Farrington et al., 2019; Pridemore et al., 2018). Some concerns – like the so-called 'file drawer problem' – are universal, so other disciplines can provide instructive guidance. For example, editors of economics journals are far more reluctant to publish replication studies that confirm the original findings than ones that overturn them, which disincentivizes researchers from pursuing these studies (Galiani et al., 2017). In a related vein, a recent survey of criminologists found that over half of those who responded to the survey – the vast majority of whom were mid-career or senior scholars – admit to underreporting results. Further, almost half admit to omitting non-significant studies or variables, which highlights the pressures to publish significant findings (Chin et al., 2023). As this pertains to replication concerns for policing survey research – and to the field more broadly – David Farrington (in Farrington et al., 2019, p. 379) called for a '*Journal of Criminological Replication*' that would publish both successful and failed replication attempts and perhaps this is a suggestion that the discipline should take seriously.

We are also faced with some unique challenges due to the sensitive nature of some of the topics we study, and the access required to study them. As is true for many subfields within criminology and criminal justice, data collection from law enforcement often requires explicit access and permission from those in charge of the agency. Thus, it is difficult and time consuming to collect primary data from police officers in a single department. And, no doubt, it is markedly more challenging to carry out officer-level data collection across multiple departments. To suggest that this be the standard for research on officer attitudes and behavioral intentions would preclude scholars from undertaking valuable research. That said, when researchers are able to collect data from officers in multiple agencies for the same study, there are minimum reporting standards that they should follow about both the samples themselves (see Nix et al., 2019) and with the analyses pooled and disaggregated by department whenever possible (see Shupard & Kearns, 2019 for an example). The current prevailing practice of simply controlling for agency with dummy variable(s) can – and does – mask important differences between departments. To be clear, we are not suggesting that scholars should *not* control for agency in their regression analyses. Rather, we suggest that they include supplemental analyses that disaggregate samples by agency to examine whether their findings are invariant across departments, which contributes to the burgeoning replication efforts within policing research and criminology and criminal justice more broadly.

Notes

1. https://www.cos.io/about/mission.
2. In some cases, the corresponding author had moved to a different institution, so we contacted those individuals at their current place of employment.
3. Jones, J.M. (2015). In U.S., confidence in police lowest in 22 years. Gallup. Retrieved from: http://www.gallup.com/poll/183704/confidence-police-lowest-years.aspx.

Acknowledgments

We thank Hyunin Baek, Carol Ann Sharo, Brandon Tregle, and Taylor Windsheimer for providing invaluable research assistance on this project. We are grateful to the studies' original authors for providing additional analyses so we could conduct the comparisons found in this manuscript. We are also grateful to Dick Adams who, when we requested additional analyses from his 2002 article, tracked down the floppy disks on which the data were saved and enlisted the help of a colleague to convert the SAS files to SPSS. Unfortunately, the data and syntax could not be recovered – but the willingness to help is commendable.

Disclosure statement

No potential conflict of interest was reported by the authors.

ORCID

Erin M. Kearns http://orcid.org/0000-0002-7895-9129
Justin Nix http://orcid.org/0000-0002-3812-8590

References

Bates, L. J., Antrobus, E., Bennett, S., & Martin, P. (2015). Comparing police and public perceptions of a routine traffic encounter. *Police Quarterly*, *18*(4), 442–468. https://doi.org/10.1177/1098611115589290

Blaskovits, B., Bennell, C., Huey, L., Kalyal, H., Walker, T., & Javala, S. (2018). A Canadian replication of Telep and Lum's (2014) examination of police officers' receptivity to empirical research. *Policing & Society*, *30*(3), 276–294. https://doi.org/10.1080/10439463.2018.1522315

Bohannon, J. (2015). Many psychology papers fail replication test. *Science*, *349*(6251), 910–911. https://doi.org/10.1126/science.349.6251.910

Chan, J. (1996). Changing police culture. *The British Journal of Criminology*, *36*(1), 109–134. https://doi.org/10.1093/oxfordjournals.bjc.a014061

Chin, J. M., Pickett, J. T., Vazire, S., & Holcombe, A. O. (2023). Questionable research practices and open science in quantitative criminology. *Journal of Quantitative Criminology* *39*(1), 21–51.

Chu, D. C., & Sun, I. Y. (2014). Reactive versus proactive attitudes toward domestic violence: A comparison of Taiwanese male and female police officers. *Crime & Delinquency*, *60*(2), 216–237. https://doi.org/10.1177/0011128710372192

Crank, J. P. (1990). The influence of environmental and organizational factors on police style in urban and rural environments. *The Journal of Research in Crime and Delinquency*, *27*(2), 166–189. https://doi.org/10.1177/0022427890027002004

Darroch, S., & Mazerolle, L. (2013). Intelligence-led policing: A comparative analysis of organizational factors influencing innovation uptake. *Police Quarterly*, *16*(1), 3–37. https://doi.org/10.1177/1098611112467411

Darroch, S., & Mazerolle, L. (2015). Intelligence-led policing: A comparative analysis of community context influencing innovation uptake. *Policing & Society*, *25*(1), 1–24. https://doi.org/10.1080/10439463.2013.784312

Domingues, I. P., & Machado, J. C. (2017). The loosely coupled factors of organizational stress in police forces. *Policing: An International Journal of Police Strategies & Management*, *40*(4), 657–671. https://doi.org/10.1108/PIJPSM-08-2016-0128

Farrington, D. P., Lösel, F., Boruch, R. F., Gottfredson, D. C., Mazerolle, L., Sherman, L. W., & Weisburd, D. (2019). Advancing knowledge about replication in criminology. *Journal of Experimental Criminology, 15*(3), 373–396. https://doi.org/10.1007/s11292-018-9337-3

Francis, G. (2012). The psychology of replication and replication in psychology. *Perspectives on Psychological Science, 7*(6), 585–594. https://doi.org/10.1177/1745691612459520

Fyfe, J. J. (1988). Police use of deadly force: Research and reform. *Justice Quarterly, 5*(2), 165–205. https://doi.org/10.1080/07418828800089691

Galiani, S., Gertler, P., & Romero, M. (2017). *Incentives for replication in economics (No. w23576).* National Bureau of Economic Research.

Gaub, J. E., Choate, D. E., Todak, N., Katz, C. M., & White, M. D. (2016). Officer perceptions of body-worn cameras before and after deployment: A study of three departments. *Police Quarterly, 19*(3), 275–302. https://doi.org/10.1177/1098611116653398

Gracia, E., García, F., & Lila, M. (2014). Male police officers' law enforcement preferences in cases of intimate partner violence versus non-intimate interpersonal violence: Do sexist attitudes and empathy matter? *Criminal Justice & Behavior, 41*(10), 1195–1213. https://doi.org/10.1177/0093854814541655

Inbar, Y. (2016). Association between contextual dependence and replicability in psychology may be spurious. *Proceedings of the National Academy of Sciences, 113*(34), E4933–4934. https://doi.org/10.1073/pnas.1608676113

Ingram, J. R., Weidner, R. R., Paoline, E. A., III, & Terrill, W. (2014). Supervisory influences on officers' perceptions of less lethal force policy: A multilevel analysis. *Policing: An International Journal of Police Strategies & Management, 37*(2), 355–372.

Ivkovich, S. K., & Khechumyan, A. (2013). The state of police integrity in Armenia: Findings from the police integrity survey. *Policing: An International Journal of Police Strategies & Management*, 36(1), 70–90.

Jennings, W. G., Fridell, L. A., & Lynch, M. D. (2014). Cops and cameras: Officer perceptions of the use of body-worn cameras in law enforcement. *Journal of Criminal Justice, 42*(6), 549–556. https://doi.org/10.1016/j.jcrimjus.2014.09.008

Karaffa, K. M., & Koch, J. M. (2016). Stigma, pluralistic ignorance, and attitudes toward seeking mental health services among police officers. *Criminal Justice & Behavior, 43*(6), 759–777. https://doi.org/10.1177/0093854815613103

Kearns, E. M. (2017). Why are some officers more supportive of community policing with minorities than others? *Justice Quarterly, 34*(7), 1213–1245. https://doi.org/10.1080/07418825.2017.1380837

Kearns, E. M. (2020). Exploring officer views of community policing in counterterrorism. *Police Practice & Research, 21*(1), 18–32. https://doi.org/10.1080/15614263.2018.1428900

King, G. (1995). Replication, replication. *PS: Political Science & Politics, 28*(3), 444–452. https://doi.org/10.2307/420301

Lambert, A. D., & Steinke, C. M. (2015). Negative perceptions of asking for support in law enforcement: Potential impact on benefit avoidance. *International Journal of Police Science & Management, 17*(2), 134–144. https://doi.org/10.1177/1461355715583004

Lee, H. D., Collins, P. A., Hsieh, M. L., Boateng, F. D., & Brody, D. (2017). Officer attitudes toward citizen review and professional accountability. *International Journal of Police Science & Management, 19*(2), 63–71. https://doi.org/10.1177/1461355717695320

Maxwell, S. E., Lau, M. Y., & Howard, G. S. (2015). Is psychology suffering from a replication crisis? What does "failure to replicate" really mean? *The American Psychologist, 70*(6), 487. https://doi.org/10.1037/a0039400

McNeeley, S., & Warner, J. J. (2015). Replication in criminology: A necessary practice. *European Journal of Criminology, 12*(5), 581–597. https://doi.org/10.1177/1477370815578197

Muibu, D. (2022). Police officer experiences with community policing and views on counterterrorism in Somalia. *The Journal of the Middle East and Africa, 13*(4), 1–28. https://doi.org/10.1080/21520844.2022.2086391

Murayama, K., Pekrun, R., & Fiedler, K. (2014). Research practices that can prevent an inflation of false-positive rates. *Personality & Social Psychology Review, 18*(2), 107–118. https://doi.org/10.1177/1088868313496330

Nix, J., Pickett, J. T., Baek, H., & Alpert, G. P. (2019). Police research, officer surveys, and response rates. *Policing & Society, 29*(5), 530–550. https://doi.org/10.1080/10439463.2017.1394300

Nix, J., Pickett, J. T., Wolfe, S. E., & Campbell, B. A. (2017). Demeanor, race, and police perceptions of procedural justice: Evidence from two randomized experiments. *Justice Quarterly, 34*(7), 1154–1183. https://doi.org/10.1080/07418825.2017.1334808

Nix, J., Wolfe, S. E., & Campbell, B. A. (2018). Command-level police officers' perceptions of the "war on cops" and de-policing. *Justice Quarterly, 35*(1), 33–54. https://doi.org/10.1080/07418825.2017.1338743

Olsson-Collentine, A., Wicherts, J. M., & van Assen, M. A. (2020). Heterogeneity in direct replications in psychology and its association with effect size. *Psychological Bulletin, 146*(10), 922. https://doi.org/10.1037/bul0000294

Paoline, E. A., III. (2004). Shedding light on police culture: An examination of officers' occupational attitudes. *Police Quarterly, 7*(2), 205–236. https://doi.org/10.1177/1098611103257074

Paoline, E. A. (2021). (Re)taking stock: Toward a richer understanding of police culture. In R. Dunham, G. Alpert, & K. McLean (Eds.), *Critical issues in policing: Contemporary readings* (8th ed., pp. 159–186). Long Grove, IL: Waveland Press, Inc.

Paoline, E. A., III, Myers, S. M., & Worden, R. E. (2000). Police culture, individualism, and community policing: Evidence from two police departments. *Justice Quarterly, 17*(3), 575–605. https://doi.org/10.1080/07418820000094671

Pridemore, W. A., Makel, M. C., & Plucker, J. A. (2018). Replication in criminology and the social sciences. *Annual Review of Criminology, 1*, 19–38. https://doi.org/10.1146/annurev-criminol-032317-091849

Ramsey, C., & Robinson, L. (2015). *Interim report of the President's task force on 21st century policing.* Office of Community Oriented Policing Services. https://cops.usdoj.gov/pdf/taskforce/taskforce_finalreport.pdf

Reiner, R., Newburn, T. (2000). Police research. In D. K. Roy & E. Wincup (Eds.), *Doing research on crime and justice.* (pp. 343–374). Oxford University Press.

Savolainen, J., & VanEseltine, M. (2018). Replication and research integrity in criminology: Introduction to the special issue. *Journal of Contemporary Criminal Justice, 34*(3), 236–244. https://doi.org/10.1177/1043986218777288

Sherwood, C. W. (2000). Job design, community policing, and higher education: A tale of two cities. *Police Quarterly, 3*(2), 191–212. https://doi.org/10.1177/1098611100003002004

Shrout, P. E., & Rodgers, J. L. (2018). Psychology, science, and knowledge construction: Broadening perspectives from the replication crisis. *Annual Review of Psychology, 69*(1), 487–510. https://doi.org/10.1146/annurev-psych-122216-011845

Shupard, M., & Kearns, E. M. (2019). Why do officers support community policing? A cross-departmental and cross-temporal comparison. *Behavioral Sciences & the Law, 37*(6), 665–680. https://doi.org/10.1002/bsl.2444

Silver, J. R., Roche, S. P., Bilach, T. J., & Bontrager Ryon, S. (2017). Traditional police culture, use of force, and procedural justice: Investigating individual, organizational, and contextual factors. *Justice Quarterly, 34*(7), 1272–1309. https://doi.org/10.1080/07418825.2017.1381756

Simons, D. J. (2014). The value of direct replication. *Perspectives on Psychological Science, 9*(1), 76–80. https://doi.org/10.1177/1745691613514755

Skogan, W. G. (2015). Surveying police officers. In M. D. Maltz & K. R. Stephen (Eds.), *Envisioning criminology: Researchers on research as a process of discovery.* (pp. 109–118). Springer.

Sun, I. Y., & Chu, D. C. (2008). Gender differences in policing: An analysis of Taiwanese officers' attitudes. *Police Practice and Research: An International Journal, 9*(5), 431–443. https://doi.org/10.1080/15614260801980869

Telep, C. W. (2017). Police officer receptivity to research and evidence-based policing: Examining variability within and across agencies. *Crime & Delinquency, 63*(8), 976–999. https://doi.org/10.1177/0011128716642253

Telep, C. W., & Lum, C. (2014). The receptivity of officers to empirical research and evidence-based policing: An examination of survey data from three agencies. *Police Quarterly, 17*(4), 359–385. https://doi.org/10.1177/1098611114548099

Van Bavel, J. J., Mende Siedlecki, P., Brady, W. J., & Reinero, D. A. (2016). Reply to Inbar: Contextual sensitivity helps explain the reproducibility gap between social and cognitive psychology. *Proceedings of the National Academy of Sciences, 113*(34), E4935–4936. https://doi.org/10.1073/pnas.1609700113

Wentz, E., & Archbold, C. A. (2012). Police perceptions of sexual assault victims: Exploring the intra-female gender hostility thesis. *Police Quarterly, 15*(1), 25–44. https://doi.org/10.1177/1098611111432843

Westmarland, L., & Rowe, M. (2018). Police ethics and integrity: Can a new code overturn the blue code? *Policing & Society, 28*(7), 854–870. https://doi.org/10.1080/10439463.2016.1262365

White, M. D. (2001). Controlling police decisions to use deadly force: Reexamining the importance of administrative policy. *Crime & Delinquency, 47*(1), 131–151. https://doi.org/10.1177/0011128701047001006

White, M. D., Cooper, J. A., Saunders, J., & Raganella, A. J. (2010). Motivations for becoming a police officer: Re-assessing officer attitudes and job satisfaction after six years on the street. *Journal of Criminal Justice, 38*(4), 520–530. https://doi.org/10.1016/j.jcrimjus.2010.04.022

Wilson, J. Q. (1968). *Varieties of police behavior: The management of law and order in eight communities.* Harvard University Press.

Wolfe, S. E., & Nix, J. (2017). Police officers' trust in their agency: Does self-legitimacy protect against supervisor procedural injustice? *Criminal Justice & Behavior, 44*(5), 717–732. https://doi.org/10.1177/0093854816671753

Appendix

Table A1. Number of officer survey articles published 2000–2017.

	2000–01		2002–03		2004–05		2006–07		2008–09		2010–11		2012–13		2014–15		2016–17		TOTAL	
Journal	M	S	M	S	M	S	M	S	M	S	M	S	M	S	M	S	M	S	M	S
BJC	0	0	0	0	0	0	0	0	0	1	0	0	0	0	0	3	0	2	**0**	**6**
C&D	0	0	1	4	0	4	0	0	0	0	0	0	0	1	1	5	1	4	**3**	**18**
CJB	0	3	0	4	0	0	0	2	0	1	0	2	0	3	0	3	0	6	**0**	**24**
CRIM	0	2	0	4	0	0	0	0	0	0	0	0	0	1	0	1	0	0	**0**	**8**
JCJ	0	2	0	4	0	5	0	5	0	4	1	8	0	1	0	3	0	5	**1**	**37**
JRCD	0	0	0	1	0	1	0	0	0	0	0	0	0	0	0	0	0	0	**0**	**2**
JQ	1	3	0	2	0	2	0	0	0	1	0	0	0	0	0	0	2	8	**3**	**16**
IJPSM	0	2	0	0	0	0	0	7	0	12	0	20	0	7	0	7	0	14	**0**	**69**
JPCP	1	2	0	3	0	2	1	4	0	5	0	8	0	4	0	4	0	23	**2**	**55**
PPR	0	0	0	2	0	2	0	1	1	8	0	9	1	11	0	10	0	16	**2**	**59**
PQ	2	9	1	10	1	6	0	9	0	12	0	8	1	9	1	10	2	14	**8**	**87**
PJPP	0	0	0	0	0	0	0	0	0	0	0	1	0	6	0	8	0	12	**0**	**27**
PIJ	0	7	1	9	0	9	3	16	0	15	0	12	2	20	0	27	1	37	**7**	**152**
P&S	0	0	0	1	0	3	0	3	0	3	0	8	0	0	1	8	2	14	**3**	**40**
TOTAL	**4**	**30**	**3**	**44**	**1**	**34**	**4**	**47**	**1**	**62**	**1**	**76**	**4**	**63**	**3**	**89**	**8**	**155**	**29**	**600**

Note: *'M' = multiple agency survey, 'S' = single agency survey.*

Index